Feed My Sheep; Lead My Sheep

Feed My Sheep; Lead My Sheep

*A Handbook of Leadership Formation
for Individuals and Groups*

N. THOMAS JOHNSON-MEDLAND

RESOURCE *Publications* • Eugene, Oregon

FEED MY SHEEP; LEAD MY SHEEP
A Handbook of Leadership Formation for Individuals and Groups

Copyright © 2011 N. Thomas Johnson-Medland. All rights reserved. Except for brief quotations in critical publications or reviews, no part of this book may be reproduced in any manner without prior written permission from the publisher. Write: Permissions, Wipf and Stock Publishers, 199 W. 8th Ave., Suite 3, Eugene, OR 97401.

Resource Publications
An Imprint of Wipf and Stock Publishers
199 W. 8th Ave., Suite 3
Eugene, OR 97401
www.wipfandstock.com

ISBN 13: 978-1-61097-140-9

Manufactured in the U.S.A.

All scripture quotations, unless otherwise indicated, are taken from the Holy Bible, New International Version®, NIV®. Copyright ©1973, 1978, 1984 by Biblica, Inc.™ Used by permission of Zondervan. All rights reserved worldwide.

This book is dedicated to all of the people who have learned to wrestle with God through camping and retreat ministries. May your prophetic call to living the life of Jesus continue to change hearts and minds for all time.

"Jesus said to them, "Very truly I tell you, unless you eat the flesh of the Son of Man and drink his blood, you have no life in you."

—Gospel of Saint John VI, 53

"Therefore go and make disciples of all nations, baptizing them in the name of the Father and of the Son and of the Holy Spirit, and teaching them to obey everything I have commanded you. And surely I am with you always, to the very end of the age."

—Gospel of Saint Matthew XXVIII, 19, 20

"The third time he said to him, "Simon son of John, do you love me?" Peter was hurt because Jesus asked him the third time, "Do you love me?" He said, "Lord, you know all things; you know that I love you." Jesus said, "Feed my sheep.""

—Gospel of Saint John XXI, 17

Contents

Preface ix
Acknowledgments xi
Introduction xiii

PART ONE THE HEART OF THE LEADER

1 Love 3

2 Joy 8

3 Peace 13

4 Patience 17

5 Kindness 21

6 Goodness 25

7 Faithfulness 29

8 Gentleness 34

9 Self-Control 38

10 Poverty of Spirit 42

11 Mourning 46

12 Meekness 50

13 Hungering and Thirsting for Righteousness 54

14 Mercifulness 58

15 Purity of Heart 62

16 Peacemaker-Ship 66

17 Persecuted for Righteousness 70

Part Two The Mind of the Leader

18 Wisdom 77

19 360° Surveillance 81

20 Goals and Priorities 85

21 Vision 89

22 Encouraging Others 93

23 Confrontation 98

24 Consistently Recharging 102

25 Celebrating Failure and Success 106

26 Honesty and Believability 110

27 Communication 114

28 Focus 119

29 Innovation 123

30 Circumambution 127

31 Servant Leadership 131

32 Managing Risk 135

33 Understanding SWOT 139

34 Paying Attention to Space 143

35 Working With and As a Team 147

36 Time Management 151

37 Interpersonal Relationships 157

38 Problem Solving 162

39 Integrity 166

40 Decision Making 170

Preface

There are a lot of books about leadership out there. I wanted to stir the pot and make some suggestions that I have not heard yet.

Leadership is not about sticking qualities all over yourself—like dozens of "yellow sticky notes". "Today I will learn time management. Tomorrow I will develop integrity." Mere information is not enough to change us. Data may lead to transformation, but it is not enough to transform us on its own. Leadership is not about "trends" and "buzzwords". Leadership is about PERSONHOOD. Personhood is where this transformation truly takes place.

Leadership may perseverate into any one of these things (stickies, trends, information, data, and buzzwords), but it is ultimately and ideally about personhood. This may be a philosophical category that the church has left off discussing, but it meant a lot to the ancients. We need to stir some of their depth back into our existence.

One's genuine ability to lead comes from one's genuine transformation into the kind of person that is needed for the particular form of leading at hand. Different traits will be called forth from the leader depending on the situation, place, time and people. It is the person that is the leader and not the trait or characteristic that is the leader. "Being" is critical; not just "doing". I think a lot of our current reading on leadership is simply about skill-sets. They are important discussions, but that is not all there is. Do not get me wrong, I am not saying you must be perfect to lead. I would not be able to write this book. I am saying that your identity is where your true leading comes from, and if you are in a transformational relationship with Jesus the chances are good that your person and identity will deepen over time.

The aim of this book is to stimulate dialogue and even argument on a philosophical level as well as a pragmatic one. The purpose is to dredge up worthwhile silt from the depths of our being and to craft it into something. It is to experience a wrestling transformation in Jesus and a deepening of your person.

Being a Christian leader is about being transformed by Jesus; becoming a new person. It is also about using tools at your disposal. For too long we have been obsessed with the checklists of leadership and its structure. Being a leader is being someone who meets with God—is torn asunder—and then brings others into that meeting—to be torn asunder. It requires a ton more, but it always requires at least this.

Look around you. Have you seen anyone torn asunder by God lately? Our churches are a shambles. Go ahead and ask pastors how much time they spend with Jesus. Ask a clergy the last time they were ravished by God. Church as we know it has destroyed our ability to be transformed by the maker of the universe. It has lost its true ability to be called out into the wilderness and be led. It is time to get rent asunder.

On one hand you are holding just another bunch of "pragmatic stickies" listing off all the things in a leader's tool box. On the other hand you are holding some questions about developing and enriching your personhood and identity, rooted in the timelessness and immutability of God. Wrestle with this stuff so you are deepening as a person. Explore the complexity of character and place in your life. Don't just make to do lists! Meet up with God and be changed. That is the ultimate journey of the leader: *"able to meet God and live; they take others to the same meeting-place."*

Acknowledgments

A SPECIAL THANKS TO Mike Kroll, Jen Foster, Meg Williams, Allen Keller, Bob Rohlfing, Bob Floyd, Matt Miles, Zachary Aidan Johnson-Medland, Josiah Gabriel Johnson-Medland and Lisa Walzer-Delgado for their feedback at the outset of this project.

Thank you also to those spiritual authors and directors/friends who over time have helped to form me in this vocation of love: Pat Woolever, Bruce Woolever, Lou Bugno, Heidi Joos, Ivy Booth, Glenn Walsh, John Lutz, Father Andrew Campbell, Brother Andrew Colquhoun, Brother Bede Mudge, Father Thomas Keating, Father Richard Rohr, Father Louis Merton, Father Basil Pennington, and Father Teilhard de Chardin. Without you leading me to Jesus, I could never have made it this far. Thank you for your writings or relationships. They have carried me over the years.

Thank you to my family: Glinda Gay, Zachary Aidan, and Josiah Gabriel. Without your ongoing love and forgiveness, I could not grow and flourish. You are my nourishment. I feed on you in my heart with thanksgiving.

A special thanks to the National United Methodist Camp and Retreat Committee for all of the hard work they do to maintain the integrity, forward motion, and spiritual development of camping and retreat ministries and professionals. And, to Pocono Plateau Camp and Retreat Center for the faithfulness to Jesus' Good News they have upheld throughout the years (I accepted Jesus there 36 years ago—1975). Both organizations have produced an endless train of leaders for Jesus and His kingdom. The proceeds of this book are being shared with both of these organizations.

Introduction

Leadership Development and Spiritual Direction/Formation

It is the premise of this book that every Jesus-follower must be about the task of meeting Jesus often and exploring their own individual identity, the identity of Jesus, and their mutual relationship. This meeting enables the deepening of the connection to Jesus and His Person. This will draw the disciple further into relationship with the Triune God and over time shape them into the ***image and likeness*** of the invisible God (this concept of image and likeness has deep theological roots and debate in the early church—much theology has been written on it).

The Jesus-follower must also be about the task of leading others into this type of relationship with Jesus, and subsequently the Trinity. This meeting and transformation is what deepens the personhood of the individual and shapes it into the ***image and likeness*** of Jesus. It is my belief that this transformation of the person is what over time molds one into the leader that will be used by God for specific purposes. It is this transformation that is the goal of the work we do in this book. One cannot simple mimic these traits. One must wrestle with them and explore them in Jesus and in one's own self—***to become a new person.***

The center of what it means to be alive is coming to terms with reality and then living within that reality. As much as we are able to do that, then we are "that much" conscious of the life we live.

For the Christian, this means meeting Jesus and living with Him to the point of our transformation. Everything else gets filtered through this "one thing". Jesus is the center.

I know that sounds so simple, so basic. But, although it is, it is not. Knowing Jesus is a bit tougher than knowing Henry, or Sally. Jesus is not just some two dimensional cut-out prophet. He is God from all ages unto all ages, which requires a certain amount of "pre-existence" and "eternalness" to pull that off. That is where it gets tricky.

It may be simple to meet Him and live with Him, but the Him that we are meeting and living with is "wild", "untamed", and "uncontainable". He is a person and personhood sustains a certain amount of depth and complexity. And, being in His Presence over time requires our ultimate transformation. It may take forever to root out some sins (boy do I know that) or learn how to resist temptation, but continual basking in His Presence (which is eternal and ineffable) will ultimately require our hearts to hunger for removing all things from our lives that keep us from being just like Him. Being with Jesus regularly demands our being made new.

Having a relationship with a pre-existent and divinely immutable Son of God sort of deepens the challenge. It makes it something that we will always be growing into, just like an expanding universe or imploding star. So, although we may be able to claim our meaning comes from meeting and living with the Son of God, when the nature of that Son of God is always just beyond our reach, comprehension, and imagination, then we are always running around to catch up with the simplicity of our own living. We always have reason and terms of growth.

In an earlier book—Cairn-Space (Johnson-Medland, Wipf and Stock Publishers, 2011), I spent time talking about "mirror" neurons. These neurons in the body imitate and adapt to the immediate surroundings and environment in order to keep us alive and relevant. Just like a chameleon, we have active cells in us that are trying to make us blend.

"Scientists have discovered a whole "mirror" system within us. The mirroring begins with the "mirror neuron" which assumes the behavior and emotion in the immediate environment and then reflects it. Individuals mirror "the other" as if it were themselves. It is how we pick up feelings of conflict and dis-continuity. If someone is saying something with their mouth that they are in conflict with in their heart, their body language will relay that information to us and our mirror neurons will pick up the disconnect. It is that feeling that something does not ring true or is just a bit off" (Johnson-Medland, Cairn-Space, Wipf and Stock, 2011, p. 36).

It goes without saying that the blending we do in order to survive happens at a sub-conscious level. It happens at a cellular level. We become a mirror of what we spend time with. This is how our personhood is established in Jesus. The more time we spend with Him, the more we mirror Him. It is that whole notion related in the stories and teachings about marriage—two flesh become as one. When you are around something over time, you eventually merge with it—at some level. Spending time with Jesus will help us mirror Him.

The center of leadership development in the Church is a relationship with this impossibly-deep Jesus. Meeting with Him in the Word, in prayer, in song, in worship, in sacrament, in silence, in centering/contemplative prayer, and in ecstatic love is the first and most vital step toward becoming a "new" person. It is also the most vital step in becoming the leader He is calling you to become. Jesus is central. Jesus is eternal, too! We will mirror what we gravitate toward.

Jesus not only calls us into relationship with Him, but He calls us to share that relationship with others. We are graced to participate in His calling others unto Himself. Jesus calls us to Himself and He asks us to lead others to Him as well. Because of this, all of us are called to leadership at some level.

We are Jesus-lovers and Jesus-leaders; those who are in relation with Him. Jesus is at the center. We go to Him and we bring others to Him. Because this Jesus is not some simple, measurable commodity that we can just deliver up and be done with, our relationship with Him will be as eternal as is His person. He is immutable, uncircumscribable, and unattainable God. He is the center. That center is endless.

The idea of spiritual formation in the life of a "new" person (a Jesus-lover/leader) begins with this daily connection. This is our first step. We meet with Jesus. We connect. We give love, words, adoration, praise, silence, centering/contemplative prayer, and song to Him; and we receive back His grace, wisdom, mercy, compassion, forgiveness and salvation. We somehow connect with and bask in His eternalness and stay open to His apophatic nature. We dialogue on who He is and who we are. We connect daily.

This is not only our first step (because He is endless); it is really our last step as well. Everything is centered in this meeting. From beginning to end, it all happens because of our encounter with Jesus: the Pre-Existent, Eternal Logos. He is God and man and wants to meet with us. He wants us to share "how to meet with Him" with others. In the realm of physics, these meetings are local encounters of the non-local. Heaven comes to bear on earth, each time we engage ourselves with God. We grow into "eternalness" in our understanding and ability to understand who this "wild" God-man truly is.

As this daily connection continues, Jesus will call us to growth through the prompting of the Holy Spirit in our lives. His personhood will demand transformation in our lives. We will want to become like Him.

Jesus wants to nurture the fruit of this Spirit (that the Father planted in us) in our HEART. He wants to give us of Himself, so we have all we need. The Fathers and Mothers of the early Church said that we are to become "by grace" (that means because Jesus gives it to us) what Jesus is "by nature". We are to become the beloved sons and daughters of God.

In this process of spiritual formation we are all becoming members of the divine family. We are becoming "little-Christs". The first step is about hooking up with the Father, in Jesus, by the Holy Spirit. At some level we will have to begin to explore the nature of Christ in studying how the believers of the past have understood His person and nature. We will digest the scriptures and theology in order to press on in a deepening understanding of the person of Jesus in and for the life of the world. But remember, the data and information is not enough. We must be transformed into His image and likeness if we expect the person of Jesus to have impacted our person.

We come to God: Father, Son, and Holy Spirit. He builds in us a new heart. Then, He wants us to bring others to Him as well—so He can rebuild them. He wants to make all things "new". Jesus is central. Keep in mind that this Jesus that is central is also endless in His existence. This assures us that our growth and need for growth will be endless and beyond measure as well. Just because Jesus is central does not make the journey to Him and living with Him an easy proposition. I stand with Bonhoeffer on this point: you have to give up everything in order to go this route. A relationship with Jesus is free, but it costs you everything you have got. You must ultimately cease to be separate from Him.

The whole depth of nature in Jesus ensures us that a lifetime itself is not enough to become intimate and joined with the Savior. It will take forever. The character that is developed in the endless process of meeting with Jesus is a character that is changed over time by the Presence of God. Like Moses' face (shining with an interior light) after visiting with the theophany of God in the burning bush, our lives take on a new stature and projection. Our nature changes gradually over time. We are made like Him. This is why the spiritual life is really about direction and formation—these words betray the process nature of our life in Christ.

This transformation is really the building of "personhood". It is in this personhood and transformation that an individual becomes a new creature that is used by God as He pleases. So, in a sense the nature of our leadership abilities rise up out of our meetings and transformations with Jesus. On one hand they are things we cannot simply discuss and learn. But, pragmatically we know that we must give some meaning to understanding our own development.

THE COMMISSIONS TO FEED AND LEAD

Jesus told us to feed on Him. Whether you believe Holy Communion is a sign and symbol; or you believe the Eucharist is the Body and Blood of Christ, you cannot escape the reality that Jesus asked us to sup with and on Him (somehow). And, He told us we could not have eternal life without doing this.

We must somehow bring Him into us and allow Him to change us into Him. That is what spiritual formation is all about. The language may shift and turn from denomination to denomination; from community to community, but the process is one and the same—we are to become "little-Christs". Jesus commissioned us to feed on Him.

Jesus told us to lead others to Him. There is this other commission that Jesus gave us (we spoke about it already), He asked us to go into the world and teach and baptize. Basically He is asking us to lead for Him. He is asking us to lead people to Him. Lead people to Him and help them learn to sup on and with Him.

He even made it plainer. He built this into yet another commission He gave to us. He asked us to feed His sheep. So we have this whirling mass of commissions from Jesus to feed on Him, lead others to Him and teach them to feed on Him. The whole process of being made "new" is about feeding (on Jesus) and leading (others to Jesus). Feeding and leading are at the core of the Gospel message. They are at the core of what we are going to take a look at here in this book. It is all about feeding and leading. Feeding on an eternal Jesus. Leading to an eternal Jesus.

In the first half of this book we are going to explore the fruit of the Spirit in our lives (a blend of the Fruit of the Spirit and the Beatitudes) and how these character traits are vital in our formation as feeders on and leaders of God. What do they have to offer us and what do they demand from us? How are they present in the life of our Jesus? We will do this by reading a discussion on each of the fruit and then spending some time with a series of workbook questions designed to help us look deeper into that particular fruit of the Spirit.

The fruit of the Spirit in our lives reveals our heart. The fruit of the Spirit are about learning to develop and receive the heart Jesus wants you to have. This first portion of the book is about the "Heart of the Leader". You will find that many of the fruit the Spirit has brought to harvest in our lives are very similar; with only slightly nuanced differences between them (for example, goodness and kindness are very similar). That is how it is in the heart. We sense the nuances in our depth.

Once we have gone through the fruit of the Spirit we will go through a list of character traits that are critical competencies for people learning to lead. That will be the focus of the second half of the book. What other things do you need to know to lead? What makes up the skill set of leaders? What is the "Mind of the Leader"? Keep in mind (and heart) that it is not simply the buzzing through tomes of information that changes us. It is in wrestling over this material with and in Jesus that transforms us. And, just because we wrestle with Jesus over this information at this stage of life, does not mean it is over and done with. As we uncover deeper layers of our personhood, we may have to re-transform areas of our lives in Jesus again.

We are all learning to lead. Even in those who are what appear to be "born leaders" there are clear needs and deficits that must be "mined and refined" so they can lead into their own leading. Without development and education no one moves ahead. This whole thing called life is a process.

In the "Heart of the Leader" we will look at:
- Love
- Joy
- Peace
- Patience
- Kindness
- Goodness
- Gentleness
- Faithfulness

- Self-Control
- Poverty of Spirit
- Mourning
- Meekness
- Hunger for Righteousness
- Mercifulness
- Purity of Heart
- Peacemaker-ship
- Persecution for Righteousness

Each fruit will have a discussion section, a toolbox section, and a workbook section. It is designed to help you work through finding out what lies at the core of each fruit and how to open yourself for the development of that fruit in your heart. Learn and interact. The workbook sections are posted on a special website (http://feedmysheepleadmysheep.blogspot.com/) designed just for this book. You can go there and download the workbook selection that you and your group are working on and either fill it out digitally or on paper format.

The second section of the book will be much the same. It will, however, deal with the qualities of the "Mind of the Leader". There will be a discussion section, a toolbox section, and then a workbook section for each of the qualities presented (http://feedmysheepleadmysheep.blogspot.com/). The goal is much the same: to find what lies at the core of these qualities and how to open up for the development of these qualities in our mind.

In the Mind of the Leader we will look at:
- Wisdom
- 360° Surveillance
- Goals and Priorities
- Vision
- Encouraging Growth
- Confrontation
- Consistently Recharging
- Celebrating Failure and Success

- Honesty and Believability
- Communication
- Focus
- Innovation
- Circumambulation
- Servant Leadership
- Managing Risk
- Understanding SWOT
- Paying Attention to Space
- Working With and As a Team
- Time Management
- Interpersonal Relationships
- Problem Solving
- Integrity
- Decision Making

The format for each section of the workbook pages will be the same in both halves of the book. I have foreshortened the spaces for answering in the workbook sample (below) for the introduction; you will have ample space to write when you get to the workbook section for each of the separate chapters. This is just a sample so you understand where we are headed. It looks like this:

FEED MY SHEEP; LEAD MY SHEEP/WORKBOOK

1. Make sure you meet with Jesus in the Word, in prayer, in song, in worship, in sacrament, silence, centering/contemplative prayer, and in ecstatic love. This is the first and most vital step toward becoming a "new" person. Write about this encounter today:
2. Today's Fruit/Leadership Quality(list):
3. Talk about Jesus and His connection to this Fruit/Quality:
4. List 5 Examples from of this Scripture (people who exhibited this Fruit/Quality):
5. List 5 Examples from your friends (people who exhibit this):

6. Spiritual Principles (list principles of this Fruit/Quality):
7. What I need to pray for to better personally enact this Fruit/Quality:
8. Google this Fruit/Quality and find an article or some social media. Read up on it. What did you find:
9. Write an essay on what you think about this Fruit/Quality after doing all of the above:
10. What goals do you have for deepening your ability in this Fruit/Quality:
11. How will this Fruit help you FEED and LEAD:

The workbook sections of this handbook are critical tools in helping us to not only enhance our understanding of the fruit and qualities of leadership, they are also a record of our interaction with these ideas and attributes. They are sort of like journal entries. They are posted online at http://feedmysheepleadmysheep.blogspot.com/ for you to download, print and fill out at your leisure. Be sure to keep them with your book and journal for group discussions.

They should not be ripped through one a day, but should be mulled over and ruminated over—massaging their meaning into our person with the help of Jesus. We are creating a map of where we are going and have been with these entries—do not rush.

The individual sections are not meant to be exhaustive tomes on each trait or quality. They are simple discussions meant to elicit and stimulate an interior conversation for the individual and an exterior conversation for the group. These conversations will themselves become processes that activate and propel us forward into growth and deepening. The inner and outer chatter should lead us and challenge us into new territory in our lives.

I am not going to fill each topic with biblical proof and theological footnotes. I will paint with broad brush strokes. Part of your journey in leadership is to make these ideals your own, so you will add to the material the depth that you want. As you do, you will be cementing the qualities into your heart and mind with all the more honesty and integrity of one who has battled with truth.

One of the greatest tools of mankind is our ability to develop and use language. It not only enables us to communicate with ourselves and others in the now, but with the advent of written language and documentation, we can study our own communications over time. As a people and as individuals we can chart our growth and development because we have written and retainable clarification of where we have been in our thinking and actions throughout time. We can record information and then we can look back over it at a later point. When we do this, we become amazed at our own depth; we have a "view onto" our own lives.

Find a special journal to work in on a regular basis throughout the journey. Maybe you can find a leather one with replaceable inserts or a large hardbound one. It will get a lot of use. You will need it for each toolbox section. I would also recommend reading my article on journaling to get a sense of the value and depth of this spiritual habit in the path of formation and direction: http://tjm-spiritualdirectionandformation.posterous.com/journaling-15 .

This powerful tool enables us to take courage and see where we have been and how we have grown. This can be encouraging to us. We often forget the vast amount of distance we cover in life—just how far we have progressed as individuals and a species. These written tracks will help us to find our way. They are our path in.

They are also wonderful discussion points for groups of people to gather around. It is suggested to use this book in a group setting so that you may benefit from the great value of listening to other peoples' interactions with the same material and issues. Knowing how someone else deals with and relates to this information will actually provide you with new insights into opening yourself to the heart and the mind of leadership. It will also teach us how community enables a deepening understanding of the mystery and identity of Jesus. The person of Christ is for the community.

A word about using this material with older youth: Although some of these concepts may be shared with older youth, the discussions may reach out into conceptual forays that will be irrelevant to them. Be mindful and discerning with how you help them hear this material. I would suggest young adults and adults talk through some of the discussion material directly with the youth (but make sure you work on these issues ahead of time by and with yourselves before you attempt to integrate them for the youth)—as you read it aloud together. Then, allow them the freedom of completing the toolbox and workbook sections on their own for future discussion. Primarily I see this material as most helpful for college age and above.

As you see how individuals (regardless of their age) interpret the topic and material (via their responses to the toolbox and workbook) you will be able to make greater strides in highlighting the attainable data from the discussions. I do not believe in *"dumbing down for kids"* as I think the stretching they do—the reaching—to try and understand larger concepts is critical in their neural development and in the accruing of their abilities used to make connections between ideas and reality. But, you must pay attention to how they are relaying information back to you about their understanding of the concepts. Monitor the work you do for effectiveness.

Even if you only gather with one other person, make sure that you expand your horizons by reviewing the materials with someone else on a routine and regular basis. May God bless you as you delve into the heart and mind of leadership in His kingdom.

Remember these chapters are only small offerings on the topics they discuss. They are seeds to be planted, watered, and nurtured. They are meant to stir some hunger in you to find out more. If you do not reach beyond these words to wrestle and grapple with God in your development as a feeder and leader then you will not grow. You will die a parrot of words; an imitator of things you do not possess in your own person—in your own self. Get ready to struggle. Get ready to grow.

In closing let me give a personal word of summation. I know our ongoing desire in this modern age to condense, align, and merge things to find stream-lined mechanisms to interpret and understand mass quantities of data and information. We like to make things simple and memorable. So, if you are looking for a way to encapsulate the themes behind the key traits in the heart and mind of a leader, let me suggest one that I think emerges from history itself.

All through the history of mankind love and wisdom have been valued as key traits and attributes. Whether we are talking about God, Truth, or humanity, these virtues emerge as the kings of virtue in the heart and mind. The heart has love and the mind has wisdom.

I will add to them one that is not in the list of either the heart or the mind, it is one that stands above them both and for them both: "discrimination". The Neptic Fathers of the church and the ecstatic mystics of the East all speak of this "crest-jewel" of discrimination ("Viveka

Chudamani" of Shankaracharya) or discernment (the "diakrisis" of the Philokalia). Being able to choose, discriminate, and discern is the highest jewel in the crown of what it means to be human. The ability to choose whether—as a leader—to respond from the heart or the mind comes from discernment. The ability to choose one trait of the heart and mind over another comes from discernment. Discernment is listening to the Spirit of God for the way in which we should go. It is the gem of what it means to be a "person"; it is the ground of our "personhood".

Love and wisdom are the key virtues of the heart and mind. Discernment is crowning virtue of both the heart and the mind. It is our connection to the Spirit of God. In this connecting virtue we use every aspect of our heart, mind, soul, and body to listen to the Spirit of God - to learn what the Spirit is calling us toward.

The leader must learn discrimination and discernment above all else; that he/she may choose from among the many gifts and traits, options and directions at their disposal in leading and feeding all mankind; leading at the call of the Spirit of God.

Feed and Lead!

WORKBOOK LINK

http://feedmysheepleadmysheep.blogspot.com/

Part One

The Heart of the Leader

1

Love

ONE OF THE MOST universally identified positive human characteristics is love. It is sought after by every life affirming group of people as a core human emotion and as a quality of life indicator. If you have love in your life and can identify it, it is seen as a valuable and stabilizing thing. It brings health to us to simply be in relationships that offer and receive love. It is a form of nourishment for people. Love is a sense of belonging and acceptance that secures our inner world and gives us a level playing field in life.

Love is so much a part of our lives that we tend to take it for granted. We forget how it shapes us and molds us into people of comfort and ease. Love conquers everything that life can throw at us. When we feel loved and are able to love we are the most stable individual we can be. We are the greatest disciple we can be. The all-pervasive love of God is what saves us and gives us life itself. It also makes us feel safe in a cosmos beyond our comprehension.

Out of all of the things Jesus made clear to us in His teachings, He made "LOVE" the clearest. He told us to love and to show the world that we are His disciples—by that love. He told us to love our enemies. He told us to love God. He told us to love others as our own selves. Everything else He taught pointed toward this great reality. Many of the images of His parables paint a picture of what love looks like; the shepherd leaving the ninety-nine sheep to find the one lost sheep is a perfect example.

If Jesus were a corporation, "Love" would be His mission statement, His goal, His tag-line, His core business value and His key strategy. Love is really what it is all about. And, He does not just tell us to love. He shows us that we are to love even though people kill us. He is His own best commercial. Love—Jesus is LOVE

This ability to LOVE beyond peoples' pettiness should crack us open a bit to the complexity and eternalness of the God-man. To love the way God loves is a proposition in understanding eternity. His love has no end. If the physicists and other scientists are right and there is one unified field for everything, I am willing to bet that it is love. It pulses through everything God has created. We just tend to miss it. Love is everything.

So, we really do not need to do anything else (but then we would have no book—so we will mention a few other things that are a part of love). Love is the summation of all of the teachings of the Law and the Prophets. It is the great commandment. All of the other pieces to being a follower of Jesus and a leader among people are pieces of love. Love is the whole puzzle of life and each piece of the puzzle.

What makes love? What is love? For that we will have millions of answers. From Jesus, we know that the greatest love that exists is laying down your life. It is getting out of the way so that someone else can shine. And, it is doing that even after the person you step out of the way for kills you on a cross. That is what Jesus did.

I am not a big fan of the retributive justice theory behind certain views of the atonement. You know, the idea that Jesus died to appease an angry Father. I think the crucifixion is something we did to Jesus because we could not live with His complete love and holiness. He just eventually pissed off the wrong people and it went sour, no matter what Saint Anselm says.

The point behind the crucifixion (clearly in my humble opinion)—if there is one point behind it—is that God loves us EVEN THOUGH WE KILLED HIM. God's love is beyond. It is beyond what is normal. It is beyond the call of duty. It is beyond what we can do or think.

Our love needs to be the same. We cannot just simply write down ten things that are love, do them, and then check them off the list and say we are done. Love is only a start. Love is also the whole journey we are on. This year the ten things that we need to do to show love will be vastly different from the ten things we must do next year. But, ALWAYS, love will be about loving no matter what other people or God do to us. That is the power of crucified love. It still loves. It loves beyond love.

The love that we are called into is faithful. It returns to those in our lives again and again despite the anguish they have caused us. Jesus loved us even though we spat on Him and crucified Him. He loved Peter even though Peter denied Him. Jesus may have been disappointed in Peter for the betrayal, but His love was underneath it all. Love is the foundation of everything. When we love someone, we have a source for the energy of accepting all that they are.

Love is an acknowledgement that each person has value and worth of their own—as they are; apart from any stipulation. It is a revering of others, honoring them, and adoring them for who they are. It does not ask them to change before it is yielded to them. Love is an ability to esteem another—something or someone other than who we are.

Love often is itself the source of our loving. In its most pure manifestation in our lives, it is something that we agree toward. It is an attribute we honor and therefore espouse. It is something that we need to reach inside and decide to do. We do not simply love the people who evoke love from us; we love even those who evoke anger from us. This was what Jesus was hinting at when He told us that even sinners love those who love them.

Love is something we must choose to draw forth from all of life. And, it is something we must choose to give away. This is no easy task. We may have to resist all sorts of other feelings we have toward people in order to get ourselves to the place where we can love them, but clearly that is the place we need to get to. This can be extremely draining. Finding the energy within to hold others in an esteem that is part adoration, part kindness, part reverence, and part faithfulness will be tiring at times. But, it must be done. Love is the measure.

The woman in Saint Mark's Gospel that broke open the container of spikenard and poured it on Jesus' head, was expressing her tender adoration and extreme surrender to Jesus. She was expressing her love. The Good Samaritan was showing his kindness and concern toward the man beaten along the road to Jerusalem and left for dead. He was expressing his love. We know the stories, they are all around us. We need to make the commitment to fulfill them with each and every person in our lives. This is a massive work and sacrifice.

This love of Jesus is so well known that the Hindu saint Sri Neem Karoli Baba (Maharaj-ji) taught his disciples that they were to meditate like Jesus did. When his students asked him, "Maharaj-ji, how did Jesus meditate?" he would respond—with tears in his eyes—"He got lost in the LOVE." WOW! Maharaj-ji got it better than most church boards and committees. "He got lost in the LOVE." That attests to the endless nature of God and the love of God.

> *Leaders are able to admire deeply even when those around them do not understand. They see past the immediate in our lives. They get lost in the love.*

Connectivity Toolbox
—Stuff for your JOURNAL

- What ten things can you do today to show your LOVE (remember, this will change every time you do it). List them in your journal.
- *"The hunger for love is much more difficult to remove than the hunger for bread."*—Mother Teresa
- What did Mother Teresa mean? Discuss this among yourselves or journal about it.
- Many people attribute pink, red, or purple with the color of love. What color do you associate with love? Discuss this among yourselves or journal about it.
- Draw, paint, or sculpt "love". Discuss this among yourselves or journal about it.
- Saint Paul said that love ***"is not self-seeking."*** I Corinthians xiii, 5.
- What did Saint Paul mean? Discuss this among yourselves or journal about it.
- Imagine someone (in your mind's eye) in your life. Picture yourself showering them with respect, honor, esteem, and acceptance. Love them.
- Do this again with several more people. Include someone who is an enemy; someone with whom you are at odds.
- Spend time talking with Jesus about how He managed to love so deeply. Listen for His response. Do this more than once and journal what you hear.
- Spend some time looking at all creation and infusing it with your love. Write about that experience.
- Google "Kahlil Gibran quotes on love." Write the quotes in your journal and explain what they bring forth from your center.
- Workbook pages at: http://feedmysheepleadmysheep.blogspot.com/

2

Joy

JOY FEELS TO ME like a sense of drawn out or elongated happiness. It is not just a single happiness in a single event, but it is happiness spread out over time. It is happiness more deeply rooted. It has a more settled feel to it than simple happiness. My sons bring me joy; not just because of who they are, but because of who they have been over the whole of their lives. They implant joy in me, not just because of one event at one time (although that is true), but because of and over many events from extended amounts of time. Joy is more about the sum of the parts of something.

It also seems to me like one of the most basic of principles and emotive forces that we can choose to live in our lives. Out of all of the things in life "choosing to feel and live in joy" seems to be more easily understood as a concept. We have to choose all of the states and responses that we wish to live in and project, but joy seems to be a really concrete one that we understand our connection to and the choosing process.

I think most of us would be able to connect with joy on the level of lemonade. That age old adage about making lemonade when life gives you lemons is about learning to find a sense of delight and elation in life even when it seems that the variables you are working with are less than favorable. Can you find a sense of settled joy even when the things going on all around you—and perhaps inside you—are sour?

Like other traits and attributes in our lives, we will find that at first we need to talk ourselves into finding the joy in situations. We need to wrestle our person into our chosen proper responses. The reason for this is that we mirror the emotional responses and mindsets of those around us at a quicker rate than perhaps a cognitive one. If the people around us are grumbling and not joyful, we will automatically begin to mirror this emotional state. We can talk ourselves out of it and actually enter into a satisfied or joyful state, but it is a conscious choice with a conscious effort required.

If the people you are with are emitting joyfulness, then chances are you will begin to mirror this joyfulness. It is really important to select the communities you inhabit based on the fact that they will literally drag you down or elevate you because of the principles behind the mirroring neurons in all of us.

Kahlil Gibran talks about joy and sorrow as if they were the same cavern or channel that is carved into our lives, into our hearts. The channel that joy carves in us is also available to be filled by the waters of joy's sister—sorrow. What he is getting at is a powerful way of discussing most emotions in our lives, most character traits. Each trait and emotion has a sister trait and emotion that exists as its alter-ego or opposing face. I want to steer away from saying positive and negative because I am not talking about emotions or traits that are bad for us, simply counter to each other (I am not saying that there are not emotions that are bad for us, I am saying that there are also emotions that counter each other). Both of these emotive forces are really running along the same axis or are made up of similar, yet opposing information.

Sorrow is deeply attached to and leads to joy in our lives. It seems that when we have disruptions or losses in regard to the things that we find joy in (people, situations, events, times), then we experience sorrow. To the depth that we have joy in our lives, to that same depth we can expect to feel sorrow. We share in sorrow because we are able to experience joy.

This is a deeply complex concept and is not easy to just write off. You will have to give some thought to this idea over the long haul in life. It will appear and emerge again and again as life goes on. Take some time now to ponder the fact that the joys in your life can easily turn to sorrows when they are disturbed. Notice how sorrow is really an expression of the loss of some joy; and see how that connects them. Trace one sorrow that you had back and find out what joy it was that you had lost.

I am reminded of the simple story of Jesus weeping when His dear friend Lazarus died. He loved Lazarus. Lazarus brought Him joy. When Lazarus died, the cavern in Jesus' life that had held His joy for the friendship was suddenly flooded with sorrow. Without going through the flooding of sorrow, Jesus would not have been able to return to acknowledging the depth of joy that He had in the relationship—at some later date.

This is classic grief work. Acknowledging the depth of sorrow over the loss enables us to move freely about in the feelings of joy—at some later time—without being encumbered with or snagged on repressed sadness. Seeing its connection to joy enables us to move sorrow from the category of being a "bad" thing. Sorrow and sadness are a part of joy.

One of the things that give me joy in life is to read. Over time I have taken joyful pleasure in sitting down and cracking open a book. In fact, when I sit down to read, I can feel myself settling into a joyful feeling because "reading itself" has carved such a deep cavern of meaning in my life over the years. There are other things that do this, too: people, places, activities, foods, and even thoughts and impressions carve these same familiar channels that are linked to joy. Can you feel this in your life as I am sharing this?

There are many similar caverns in us. At some point, as we begin to discuss the character traits and emotions involved in the heart of a leader, we are going to uncover the fact life is very complex and that something we are looking at today, may look and feel very different tomorrow or at some other time in the future. Our sense of joy and what brings us joy is fluid and will shift and change over time. Just like a river winds and bends and then straightens out over time, our connection to and understanding of these things we are looking at now will change. This is ok. Part of why we are writing it down and discussing it in groups is to find ways of looking at these things from different positions.

Finding joy is the thing that should be consistent in your life. The things that trigger joy in you may be different as time goes on, but you should be able to plug into joy at any point in your life. You should be able to scour your life and find something that infuses your heart with joy. Then, you should decide that being infused with joy is such a powerful thing that you want to see it happen more often.

What if you sat down right now and asked you what infuses you with joy—right now? I bet you would look around to find something that gives you joy. When you find it, I bet your feeling within changes. But, you could also close your eyes and ask yourself the same question. What gives you joy right now? Instead of looking at the stuff around you, you may be challenged to look at some invisible things (since your eyes are closed) like relationships or things that are not in your immediate range of vision for this moment.

So, now we have two things that we can rely on to not only bolster up our heart, but even change the direction our heart is headed for this moment: love and joy. So many people think that they are poor and have no resources to do anything. Right now you can reach into your heart and find love and joy and one thousand memories and impressions that are attached to those two notions. Every one of those memories and impressions is capital in your life. Those things make you truly rich, but if you do not stop and look at them, well then you may just be the poorer for it.

One of the great sets of stories about joy that I plug into are the kingdom stories from the Gospels. These are the stories that relate the kingdom of God to some thing that is lost and then found, or is discovered and then purchased. Think of the lost coin, the lost son, the treasure in the field and the pearl of great price. When the person finds the object, everything in their life opens open. Hope and a million other things present themselves at that moment. Those stories are stories of joy. This should remind us that true joy is always attached to hope. When we find something that we deeply hope and long for, joy bursts into our lives. This reminds us that joy is attached to our sense of satisfaction and contentment. Where is your satisfaction and contentment in life rooted – what satisfies you and makes you content? What would you sell everything to obtain?

Leaders are able to find joy because they sharpen their vision and look for it harder than others.

Connectivity Toolbox
—Stuff for your JOURNAL

- List 10 or 20 things in your journal that give you joy.
- James 1:1–3 says: "*Consider it pure joy, my brothers, whenever you face trials of many kinds, because you know that the testing of your faith develops perseverance.*" Copy this in your journal.
- Journal about the depth of joy and sorrow that James is pointing us toward in the above passage.
- Do the things that give you joy help develop perseverance in you?
- Write in your journal about the connection between your own personal joys and sorrows.
- Talk to Jesus about joy and sorrow in your life. Ask Him how He wants you to deal with them. Listen for His answer and then journal about it.
- What colors represent joy for you? List them in your journal.
- What colors represent sorrow for you? List them in your journal.
- What are your current hopes and dreams in life?
- Talk to Jesus about the things that give Him joy. Journal the responses that you feel emerge from within.
- Workbook pages at: http://feedmysheepleadmysheep.blogspot.com/

3

Peace

THE WORD PEACE SHOWS up in the early church liturgies over and over again. Most every petition offered up by the deacon in church services begins with, "Again and again in peace, let us pray to the LORD." This is true not only for Eucharistic liturgies, but for most every service within the Horologion (the Orthodox Hours of Worship). It was an intentional weaving of a concept into the celebrations of the church. It was the setting of a precedent based on an ideology. This was the whole purpose of liturgy—carving out worship that set bounds on our cognitive parameters and intellectual concepts concerning the nature of God and His world: praising God and teaching us at the same time.

The word peace, as it is rendered in the liturgical settings of prayer is the Greek equivalent of the Hebrew word "Shalom". It is a word that connotes and denotes wholeness, completeness, rest, and tranquility of soul. It reaches beyond our political sense of peace, which is often nothing more than the absence of chaos, conflict, or strife. It delves into the idea that we can actively restrain or limit things in our lives that lead to disturbance and the ruffling of tranquility, in order to attain to a sense of calm. Peace is something we struggle to attain, not simply something that happens in the absence of war.

Peace is akin to the idea of "apatheia" in the Fathers of the Church. Apatheia is a "laying aside of all earthly cares" (a quote from the historic Cherubic Hymn). It is a refusal to pick up the chords of strife and discord. Apatheia is first a detachment from all that overburdens us. Eventually, we learn non-attachment; that is not getting attached to certain things in the first place. This detachment gives us space for peace.

Being in control of what we choose to attach to is a sign of spiritual maturity. At first we need to prune back all of the vines of chaos that have wrapped themselves around us, choking us out. Eventually, we learn to prune the vines before they entwine and entangle themselves around our lives.

There is a sense of spiritual struggle and choice involved in the process of peace, it is a work toward growth in salvation. Apatheia is about not being attached to too many things; about being attached at critical points to that which is worthy. Jesus.

When I think of this kind of peace I think of some real concrete steps that need to be taken to preserve its hegemony. For example, this kind of peace in our prayer life requires boundaries being set: like not answering the phone during morning and evening prayer and meditation periods in our home. It means saying no to activities on Saturday evenings so we can prepare for worship and the receiving of sacraments. It means fasting and abstaining from overt activities sometimes in our lives so that we may take up Sabbath rest and a sense of listening to God. This peace requires the struggle of discipline to attain. We need to develop strategies to maintain peace and peacefulness in our lives. What about not carrying a cell phone? What about not answering your home phone after 8:00 in the evening and before 9:00 in the morning? What about asking your kids to plan at least one week ahead for activities? What about keeping your friends on a clear schedule for getting together—like once a month we go out? All of these strategies for maintaining peace actually buy you the territory you are looking for.

When you think about the advantages that a country obtains from peace they are many. It is true with an individual as well. There are less deaths and injuries (physical and emotional). There is more money and time to devote to non-defense oriented budgets. There are advances made in many other areas of development like: space exploration, scientific discoveries, intellectual pursuits, and social reforms. These are signs of progress that a nation, city, or community experiences when they are living in an extended peace. What are the advantages and benefits that an individual and a family can reap from the overt guarding of peace in the home and in the heart? They are infinite.

Saint Seraphim of Sarov, a Russian Orthodox Saint from the 18th century saw peace as a driving force in the salvation of the world. He said that we should, "seek inner peace and thousands would be saved around us." He understood that our bringing of peace into the world would give people a clear picture of the kingdom of God and would cause them to hunger and thirst after the benefits of that kingdom. Seek inner peace.

We often think of Saint Francis when we think of peace. He was someone so calm that the animals were not afraid of him. The animals and the people came to listen to his sermons. That sort of peace comes from giving up everything to follow Jesus. The ways and wiles of a man of God are so mysterious and so peculiar to all of creation, that all of creation flocks to see them. They marvel at the peace that exudes from such folks. All you have to do to obtain that transcendent peace is to give up everything and follow Jesus. Simple, eh?

Clearly, at some point, the peace of Christ takes hold in you and you begin to find that you make decisions based on maintaining the seed of peace that Jesus has planted. You begin to guard your heart by cutting out things that take you out of the peace of God. If you are not noticing a deep craving for more peace in your life, check in with yourself to see if you are over extended and exhausted. Sometimes, when we are beyond our limits, all we want is to collapse, not to find peace. This is a good indicator that we are over-reaching our capabilities and our commitments. When you are all stretched out and over-extended, it is time to prune some things out and make room for peace. Creating space and clearing space is really good image for what peace does in us. Peace gives us room; peace gives us shelter. Where is your peace; your shelter?

Leaders value space where there is rest because they understand the healing nature of a reduction in activity and conflict. This space—both inside and out—is the fertile seedbed of peace.

Connectivity Toolbox
—Stuff for your Journal

- List five things - in your journal—that you can do to give yourself a few minutes of peace in the morning and in the evening.
- Do those things for a week and journal about the new space in your life.
- How do you think Jesus defines peace? Journal about it.
- If you were a king and you were guaranteed 10 years of peace, what 10 things would you do to take advantage of the time of prosperity? What investments would you make because of the time and resources afforded you. List them in your journal.
- What is the prosperity that comes from peace all about? How does abundance figure into that idea? Journal about this.
- What "vines" seem to be encroaching on your life and trying to choke you? List out 10—15 things (in your journal) that you feel are keeping you from attaining the identity in Christ you believe you are called to?
- How will you seek to prune those vines and detach them from your life? Journal about this.
- Which vines do you feel are the hardest to keep pruned in your life? List the things that you feel powerless to detach from.
- Spend some time with Jesus honestly talking about the areas you feel you are choking in; the areas you cannot prune out on your own. If you feel desperate, be sure not to hide that feeling from Him. Listen to what He says to you, and write it out in your journal
- Return to the words you heard Jesus say to you later in the day, later in the week. Reread them and hear what He speaks to you, again and again.
- Workbook pages at: http://feedmysheepleadmysheep.blogspot.com/

4

Patience

Patience is related to suffering. It is being able to tolerate some form of suffering over time. It is bearing with something with some greater end in mind. The "greater end" makes the suffering worthwhile enough to endure through to a conclusion or cessation. Great works of art are unleashed on the planet after artists patiently endure the process of interior germination. Giving birth to a child and raising that child to adulthood shares some of the same points of similarity with great works of art. This type of holding-endurance is patience.

Love, joy, and peace may be attributes we strive to attain and hold onto for long periods of time, but patience is something that comes and goes with situations. We can have love, joy, and peace with or without conflict, but patience only exists in us because of conflict. It is present in relation to the presence of conflict. In fact, it is patience that helps us to maintain love, joy, peace and all other good things in the midst of conflict.

Patience is discovering that holding on to the good - hoping to be good - amid the turmoil and chaos of conflict is something that we esteem and wish to accomplish. We can glide along in a state of love, or joy, or peace until conflict comes along. Then, we need to be patient to get through that period with the same depth of love, joy, and peace we had before the conflict showed up. Patience is a commitment to our core values with a hope that they are worthwhile and even better for all of us then the turmoil that has presented itself.

Because of this, it seems there is a relation between our patience and how much pain we can bear. This just means, like everything else in life, we need to grow into patience. We may start out by being able to tolerate only a little bit of confusion, chaos, and pain, but as we experience more of life we are able to bear up under a lot more adversity.

I am reminded that Jesus set the standard for us concerning the forbearing quality of patience. He told us to take up our cross and follow Him. Whatever the suffering was, He sanctified it by telling us that we should pick it up. We should carry the suffering in our lives, and be patient with and among it. We espouse patience because Jesus asked us to. He proved His commitment to the process by taking up His cross to the point of death.

So often in this techo-savy and pharmacologically adept culture we have the resources at our disposal to remove suffering. We can take away just about any pain. The question must be asked, what purpose does this suffering have in our lives, and should we mask it or alleviate it? Should we bear it? If we were to remove all of the pain from our lives we would not only absent ourselves from the soul-depth that comes from living amid suffering, we would also be lessening our bodies' contributions to the redemptive process.

In the physical realm, the suffering that comes from pain is a reminder that something is being done or is happening that is stressful for the organism. The pain of a swollen joint tells us that the inflammation is making it difficult for us to move. Pain tells us that everything is not all right. We can take away the pain with medicine, but we are also taking away the physical condition responsible for warning us to take it easy. The pain reminds us that we are injured. Without the pain, it is easy to overextend our wounded limbs and damage them further.

Father Richard Rohr, OFM told us that we will transmit our pain to others unless we transform it within ourselves. We must work with the suffering and pain in our lives in order to rise up out of it. This notion keeps us about the task of seeing how our brokenness, woundedness, and sin fit into the larger map of our existence. I am always surprised at how much the wounds in my life keep me focused on issues that are at the center of the universal life. My wounds are where I get my power to heal others; but, only when I connect with them and acknowledge their reality.

This reminds us that patience is a softening into the idea that everything is wounded and broken and nothing is antiseptically pure and unabashed. This is helpful in a society that is bent on hiding anything that looks like a failure. Such an attitude of hiding the imperfect does nothing to help us live with the compromise and alteration that comes from living amid imperfection. When we fail and learn to live amongst that failure, we are automatically gaining interior knowledge on how to cope. Someone that is deeply patient is someone who understands their own brokenness and imperfection. The patient one is compassionately aware of the cost of imperfection in the lives of others. It is this compassion that stirs them to enduring.

Most major works of art are a rendering - in a particular medium - of suffering with some idea and concept until it births itself. The idea that art comes from the Muses is perhaps deeply connected to the fact that art comes from a patient musing over what it is that is inside. Almost like the small piece of sand that irritates the inner lining of the oyster until it produces a pearl—art is nothing more than a patient wrapping of layers of meaning around an interior irritant. Working with the ability to cope over time, something great is always produced.

Is patience any different? What will you create with the suffering that is within and all about? How will you bear suffering in such a way as to redeem it? That is patience.

Knowledge is one of the things that expands our abilities to respond with patience. When we find out the greater horizons of something we are dealing with, then we are often able to suffer along a bit further. When we have little food or funds, sometimes the knowledge that others are also going through this experience (sometimes even much worse) gives us the impetus to press on with patience. When we find out that the suffering we are enduring is only short-lived; this knowledge also sets us free to relax into the experience and wait with hope.

> ***Leaders grow in their ability to be patient because they are growing in their ability to love and to hope. They allow their suffering (an irritating piece of sand) to be born into pearls of great price.***

Connectivity Toolbox
—Stuff for your Journal

- Put together a list of things (in your journal) that drive you crazy; things that make you feel as if you "have no patience" or "have lost your patience".

- List (in your journal) some things that Jesus has been more than patient with you about.

- List (in your journal) some things that you are being patient with others about.

- Overhear the story of the ungrateful servant in scripture (Gospel of Saint Matthew xviii, 21—35.) Read it and journal about how this story reflects the concepts of forbearance discussed above.

- Google some famous artists and find out how long some of their major pieces of art took them to create. Journal about this. How did they hold on so long?

- Google about the process an oyster goes through to create a pearl. Write a poem or an essay in your journal about this process.

- Journal about what color you think of when you think of patience. Why?

- What is the longest thing you have had to wait for? Was it a gift, some mail, a skill or ability? How long did you wait? What made it worth waiting for? Journal about these things.

- Write an essay about Job and the experiences of his life (in your journal). If you need help go back to the book in the bible and read it first. Talk about the different forms of patience that he applied throughout the ordeals that were visited on him.

- Workbook pages at: http://feedmysheepleadmysheep.blogspot.com/

5

Kindness

Kindness is itself a form of good-things (we shall discuss goodness itself in the next chapter). Kindness is good-things in physical form. It is good-things that come out of us in one form or another and are expressed to someone else. It may be words, wishes (thoughts expressed), or deeds. Kindness is good-things exposed in form; it is the heart itself exposed in form.

Many of our heart traits are emotions, notions, ideals, and impressions that linger in us and are reserved in us—often obscured from the view of other people. We hide our feelings, notions, ideals, and impressions. When our positive and wholesome feelings, notions, ideals, and impressions escape us and become visible, they appear as kindness and acts of kindness. Everything in us has got to reveal itself at some point (the good as well as the ill).

Our love, joy, peace, and patience will show up in our expressions toward God and others. When our heart is filled with such wonderful things (and we know it) we are left with no other option save sharing them with others. Eventually, with training, when we see how rich and full we are of the good-things of God, we will learn to share what we have. This sharing of our heart-fullness is kindness.

I remember seeing children sharing with each other at the playground while my sons were off making pretend. One child did not have a cup of ice cream, he was staring at another little boy who did. The boy with the ice cream offered a spoonful to the boy without. My eye sparkled with a glint and my heart shivered with hope. The same thing happened when some girls offered to take in a child who had no friends. They nonchalantly ushered her into the circle of their playing.

The thing about playground kindness is that it looks so natural. It seems like the right thing to do. It is an assent toward the truthful. When you take stock in that sort of charitable behavior, it makes you wonder why we would ever choose to do anything but offer nonchalant kindness. But, we know that people do chose to be mean—cruel even. You can see that behavior on the playground, too.

In either case, when we see the dramas of kindness or cruelty played out before us, we tend to have strong feelings about which is right and which is wrong. Those strong feelings are not enough, however, to empower us to act in the proper way every time. We must gradually grow toward acting with kindness in each situation by acting with kindness in some situations—slowly progressing toward more.

The acts that we equate with kindness are really reflections of the interior life and not so much of the exterior environment. This can be noted in situations that are dire and horrific. Just because what is happening all around us is chaotic and bleak, it does not mean that decent people cannot reach inside and share their good character in the shape of an act of kindness.

Stories in the Warsaw Ghettoes and in the Nazi Death Camps abound of one prisoner sharing bread with another; one dying person comforting another dying person. There are also tales of greed and superiority. What this gets at for me is that it is something intrinsic which manifests itself in the horror of the situations. Environments and situations are not soley responsible for how people will respond. There are of course shades to the grey of this type of thinking—good people can get stretched beyond their limits—but that people can exhibit any kindness at all in evil situations is worth figuring out and discussing.

The vast majority of the time we do not see a lot of acts of kindness being done; we do not perform a lot ourselves. We get all geared up and into our own individual lives and the alleged goals, demands, and aspirations that revolve around keeping ourselves alive and going. We fail and forget to reflect on the nature and depth of what we already have, of who we already are, and where we have already been. When we do pause and reflect, we are able to see the abundance which exists in even our most desperate hours of life. That abundance wells up in us and overflows—escaping the bounds of our limited self (ego). It spreads to our larger Self (the community and God).

It may take some simple planning to ask yourself, "What do I have to be grateful for?" And then, as you hear yourself respond to that question, allow yourself to notice how much you do have. Not just stuff, but love, joy, peace, grace, children, smiles, friends. Then, ask yourself, "how can I share my love, joy, peace, grace, children, smiles, friends with someone else so they can feel equally as blessed?" What can I do for my wife to show her my deep joy? What can I do for my children to show them my abundant love? What can I say to my neighbor to allow him to feel this same inner abundance in his life?

These acts of kindness move the world. When acts of kindness occur in our lives—when we are the recipient—the world slows down, we take notice, and it is cemented into our lives that someone has gone out of their way for us. Acts of kindness change who people are. They help enable people to pay it forward. They build up interior momentum that forces us to pass along similar acts and gestures. Kindness opens hearts—even those that have been welded shut.

If you want to see something magical, reach inside of your heart and mix up your love and joy and perform some simple and random act of kindness. Do something to show someone your patience. The world will never be the same again.

Leaders do not see kindness as a weakness,
but a strength that changes the world.

Connectivity Toolbox
—Stuff for your Journal

- List kindnesses (in your journal) that you have witnessed in your life that have given you pause and have impacted your heart.
- Write out 10 simple acts of kindness (in your journal) that would be easy for you to perform.
- Perform these 10 simple acts of kindness and put a check mark next to them when you have completed them (along with a name of who they were performed for).
- Copy this quote by Mother Teresa in your journal. *"Let no one ever come to you without leaving better and happier. Be the living expression of God's kindness: kindness in your face, kindness in your eyes, and kindness in your smile."*
- Journal about what Mother Teresa meant by the statement above. How is your life a living expression of God's kindness? List ways you may help it become that living expression.
- Can you imagine an act of kindness that may actually cause suffering in someone's life? Write about that scenario in your journal.
- Discuss with some other people whether the above is even possible. Would you still call that situation "kindness" or is it something else? Make notes about your discussions in your journal.
- Go back and read through your journal entries. Write about what you notice or how you feel when you read these entries.
- Workbook pages at: http://feedmysheepleadmysheep.blogspot.com/

6

Goodness

GOODNESS IS SOMETHING WE strive toward, but it is also a commodity of the soul. It comes out of us in direct proportion to its quantity within. Planted in us by the Spirit; it is ours to nurture into fullness. How will we develop the seeds of goodness that are in us? How will we tend their growth in our being?

I think removing ill thoughts is a good place for us to begin—sort of cleaning out the space around the goodness. We need to occasionally get rid of all the weeds and brambles that choke out the plants in the garden of the heart, so the soul-full vegetation of our lives may thrive into vibrancy.

It is that way with all of the gifts of the Spirit and fruit of the Spirit that are planted and nurtured within the heart. Without regular and routine pruning and weeding, any garden, arbor, or vineyard becomes a tangle of sick and compromised growth. The fruit produced is not only fractional in its quantity but the quality is marred as well. Uncared for fruit trees produce bitter and woody tasting fruit. How is the fruit of our heart to the eye and to the tongue?

I love the word "good". It is one of those words that are fun to say over and over again. And, it is a word we use over and over again; for just about anything. We may have muddied some of the meaning in its overextension of use.

The quality itself, as it is engendered in people, has its definition in "moral excellence", sort of an "ethical police" mindset. I think the word is deeper than this definition. I think the connotation of goodness is a better place for us to spend our time. That which is "good" has a certain solidness to it. It is not just "not-badness", but it is consistently "not bad". People that we consider to be "good" or "salt of the earth" are folks who we consider to be "rooted" in decency. They are not going anywhere in their goodness.

I think another word that sums up this connotation of the "good" is wholesome. It is a word that deepens and fills out the image and concept of goodness. It somehow adds another layer to the quality.

I have noticed that as we age these sorts of parallel meanings or deepening connotations occur for words and the images that those words bring into our lives. When we are young—or young in the faith—words like Jesus, Father, Spirit, salvation, redemption, forgiveness, and grace (as well as every other word and image in our lives) mean and evoke one thing. That thing that they mean is like a point on a piece of paper; singular in its appearance and small. The paper itself a field limited in size and thin in depth.

As time goes on, though, the meaning of that thing takes on a broader sense—based on an increased understanding. The dot spreads out on the page and become a circle of enlarging circumference; first the size of a dime and then the size of a quarter. The paper itself—the field of our knowing if you will—also expands in size and thickens in its depth.

Then, as we continue to develop associations with those understandings (relationships with people who help us to understand these concepts, places we go to that help us understand these concepts, as well as emotions and yearning that become attached to these meanings and concepts—things that connect one idea to another) then the circles take on three dimensional capacities and deepen through the paper and become like marbles instead of flat diagrams. The paper itself thickens to the depth of a cereal box. This goes on and on as long as we are open and continue to expand. If we shut down and choose not to develop, this process becomes frozen.

This deepening goes on with everything we know, feel, and do in life. It is why as a young child we understand "some" about life and circumstances, but as an adult we can understand "more" about these same things. We have added layers, depth, and expanded the edges of our understanding and interaction with life. All of this is based on our having encompassed more experience in our lives—more points of reference and connection.

Part of this process of growth hearkens back to the first image in this section; the image of pruning back that which is ill in order to find health in that which is good. Part of goodness is pruning out the growth that is not healthy. This is the portion of goodness that leans toward purity. The way we fortify the purity in our lives is by working on getting rid of the things that we know to be harmful, unhealthy, and tainted with disease.

Once we begin to clear away the weak and sick portions of life we can get a sense of what is left; of what makes up the good. We know that the fruit and gifts of the Spirit are portions of our life that are good. But, there are many other things as well. Rest is good. Quiet is good. Stillness is good. Solitude is good. Community is good. Worship, praise, and adoration are good. Under the brambles of chaos, confusion, and too much activity was a whole garden of good.

A leader knows that sometimes, in order to get a view of what is good in life, we have to clear out the debris and dead-wood.

Connectivity Toolbox
—Stuff for your Journal

- Copy this quote in your journal. *"All that is necessary for the triumph of evil is that good men do nothing."*—Edmund Burke
- What do you think Burke was talking about? List several examples of times this has happened in history or possible scenarios in which this could happen (in your journal).
- List features or qualities that you believe make a person good (in your journal).
- Describe what makes a worship service good as opposed to bad (in your journal). How about a family meal? A friendship?
- When you were a child, your list of things that you considered to be good was quite different from what it is today. Make a list in your journal of things that "made life good" when you were a child; and then make a list of things that "make life good" at this point in your life.
- How many things in your two lists above where the same?
- In your journal list out some things in your life that you could prune out to make your life a bit more solid, pure, or healthy. These things, if removed, would move you closer to being rooted in the good. Talk about these things with Jesus and journal anything you hear Him saying to you.
- Look through several magazines and begin a running list (in your journal) of the images of "the good life" that are presented and portrayed there. How do these mesh or clash with your own understanding of the "good life"? Share these with your group and discuss the value of these images in affecting peoples' development.
- Workbook pages at: http://feedmysheepleadmysheep.blogspot.com/

7

Faithfulness

Being faithful to something is being committed to that thing in such a way so as not to be moved away from that thing. You are rooted in that thing; you are connected to that thing; you are tied to that thing. Faithfulness is complete symbiosis—complete connection. But, it is connection by choice. And, it is connection by choice over time.

Faithfulness is not a one way phenomenon. That is, when a friend or lover is faithful to you, that does not mean they are not getting anything out of the relationship or connection. The word symbiosis was used above to fill out the image of faithfulness. We can be rooted in and tied to something we are faithful to, and at the same time be receiving from it. As a matter of fact, sometimes our faithfulness to a thing is simply because it feeds us. Now that can be a more infantile form of faithfulness, but it is faithfulness, nonetheless.

Faithfulness in the heart of a leader and feeder is what connects the leader and feeder to something over time. We can say that love is the connection, but faithfulness is connecting with that love over and over again—over time. Choosing to connect over time makes you faithful.

The finest and the best images of faithfulness come from God. When we think of some of the other traits we have mentioned we know that God exhibits them but there are times we have exhibited them as well. We have been joyful. We have loved. We have been kind. But, faithfulness, because it is about a chosen commitment *over time*, is best seen in God's relationship to us. He is eternal and has been the most faithful *over time* simply because He has been in existence over more time than we have been. But, He is also most faithful because He has not broken the connection or severed the ties, even when we killed Him.

Though we are sinful and proud, God continues to come to us, to love us, and to desire us—over and over again. Though we nailed Him to a tree when he came to be with us and walk among us, He longs to be in communion with us. He loves us in spite of our unloving attitude toward Him.

It is really something hard to wrap the mind around. I know when someone hurts me; the first thing that comes to mind is to sever ties—to sever my faithful connection. That God can be so faithful again and again and again is as awesome and mystifying to me as the fact that there are hundreds of billions of galaxies out there (which we can see thanks to the Hubble Ultra Deep Field photographs).

Bringing it down to our lives and our small little dramas in life, faithfulness in the lives of people is best imaged by a mother's devotion to tending her child. The icons of the Virgin and Child that have been a part of Christian history from about the third century on (some say even Saint Luke the Evangelist painted a Virgin and Child icon) have been an important way of passing on the idea of faithfulness between God and man. The love that passes back and forth between a mother and child is an image of the love between God and His children. Regardless of what the child does or has to offer, the mother is there to nurture the child deeper into life. The faithfulness is not based on any return for the mother from the child.

The other image of faithfulness that we speak about in human terms is the faithfulness of a husband for a wife and a wife for a husband. In this relationship the risk is much higher than the previous example. With a mother and child if the infant somehow violates a mother's trust, it is easier to accept because the child is not fully developed and does not "know better".

In the case of a spouse, we do not so easily let the spouse off the hook for unfaithfulness. We do not offer up the excuse, "They did not know any better". In these more mature relationships the stakes of faithfulness and unfaithfulness are expected to be better understood. The adult understands (or should) that the faithfulness they receive is directly connected to the faithfulness they give.

God's faithfulness is even deeper than this. God's faithfulness is more mature. He is willing to be faithful when the object of His faithfulness becomes evil, destructive, and hurtful. We see this story again and again in the life of the people of Israel and in their relation to God. God is faithful again and again. The nation of Israel is unfaithful again and again. We see this in our own lives. God is faithful; we are unfaithful.

In the story of Hosea the point is driven home wildly as we see that God remains faithful to Israel the way Hosea remains faithful to his wife who has prostituted herself. God is faithful until His children return and beyond that. God is always hungry for the faithfulness of His children. God reaches out to us as a Lover to the beloved. He is ever hopeful and ever faithful.

There are times that He disciplines Israel for their behavior. He does the same with all His children. There are times when He "sends them out", but He never changes His faithfulness. He does not take a new nation—a new people—to be His own. He longs for no other Bride.

We must be careful here. The text is not about nationalism and who God has chosen—over and against a people that He has not chosen. It is about the fact that God is faithful to His children. In the advent of the new covenant we have with God, His children are all those who turn to Him, long for faithfulness with Him, and return to Him when they are unable to be faithful. The children of God try to become as faithful to Him as He is to us.

So, we need to look at our faithfulness to God, recognize our key points of failure, and how it is we catch ourselves; learning to return to Him once we have failed. How do we approach God when we have been unfaithful to Him?

As leaders and feeders we should look at a few levels of faithfulness in our interactions with others. What level of faithfulness do we hold ourselves to in regard to others? What does that mean and or look like? How do we handle people being unfaithful to us, to the group or to Jesus? Does our response to peoples' unfaithfulness model God's response to unfaithfulness? If not, how will we get our response to match God's?

Faithfulness rests on a strong and foundational understanding of how to return to a faithful relationship once one has become unfaithful. It also rests on a solid commitment to forgiveness and grace. Just as the Father extends these things to us (think of the father running to greet the returning prodigal son) we must become familiar with being able to extend these things to the communities we engender in trying to feed on Jesus in our hearts and lives.

We need to be able to make people feel at ease when they return after having been unfaithful. We need to echo God's firm and unconditional love. Our ability to impart some of God's faithfulness to others will be a sure example of His grace and forgiveness in their lives.

> *A leader understands that faithfulness will always be broken and is sure and clear in helping people know how to return to a full and faithful relationship again. A leader is able to help people feel loved and longed for when they do return.*

Connectivity Toolbox
—Stuff for your Journal

- List ten ways (in your journal) you are faithful to people in your life.
- List ten ways (in your journal) that people in your life are faithful to you.
- Where are you the most faithful in your life? Write about it and discuss it with the group?
- Journal as if you were Hosea? Write about the type of suffering you would be experiencing knowing that your lovely wife was prostituting herself throughout Israel.
- List ways that God tolerates your "prostituting of yourself" to things that are not of Him?
- Copy this quote (by Edwin Louis Cole) in your journal: *"Confidentiality is a virtue of the loyal, as loyalty is the virtue of faithfulness."*
- Write about the meaning of the above quote in your journal.
- How did Jesus deal with the woman caught in adultery? Journal your answer.
- What does this say about how God deals with us when we are unfaithful? Talk to Jesus about how He has done this for you in the past. Journal your answer and anything you hear Jesus sharing with you in your conversation.
- Workbook pages at: http://feedmysheepleadmysheep.blogspot.com/

8

Gentleness

When I think of gentleness my mind always flashes back to standing under a maple tree in my front yard at the age of eight. I am standing in the sun, hands cupped together and in front of my chest, holding a delicate but unbroken robin's egg. The small blue egg was lying on the ground, unharmed by the process that got it there. I remember how gingerly I held it; thinking I could keep the fragile life inside alive until it hatched. I could not. But, this has always been in me as what gentleness is about. I was reserving and conserving the strength I had in order to keep this life safe.

Gentleness entails protective measures and acts to sustain something that may or may not be fragile. We keep ourselves from acting with whatever full force we are capable of, in order to honor and sustain—nurture even—something within our grasp. It may be a friend, a relationship, an emotion, a fawn—it does not matter. Gentleness is somehow a curbing or a curtailing of the magnitude of interactions on "some thing" to keep it safe. It is a softening of things in order to preserve something.

Scenes like the child with a robin's egg, or with a nest call forth gentleness from within us. Babies do the same. Sick and dying people that are in bed or in a hospital room do this. When we find out someone has experienced a trauma we also get into a space of "gentleness". Many of the times that we move into gentleness we move into it almost as a reflex. Some piece of us registers that safety—at some level—is an issue and we slam on the brakes. We slow down, we speak softly, we hug, and we reach out with neutralized hands and strength because at a cellular level we see an exposed nerve or sense a fragile nature.

Scientists would tell us that our mirroring neurons perceived the data and shepherded us into an appropriate stance and response. It is all happening at the microscopic and even non-cognitive or precognitive level.

When you hold several images of gentleness together in tension, it appears that they all are doing a few things in common. First, our images of gentleness are all about creating a safe space around a person, a place, an object, an emotion, a thought, or a situation. We move things back out of the way of that specific environment. Second, the images all reveal some form of protection. They all have a component of watchfulness in them that is tuned toward keeping the environment safe. Third, they tend to have some continuation of the "safe space" and "protection" motifs by nurturing the environment into the future; keeping things safe for an extended period of time. All of our gentleness entails creating safe space, protecting, and nurturing.

What is interesting about gentleness is that in order to provide these three things—let us say—for a baby bird, we are willing to go ballistic on the neighbor's dog that runs toward us with the intent to eat the bird in our hands. We protect one thing by posing force toward another thing that threatens the first thing. We "knee" the dog in order to save the bird. So there is some acknowledgement that gentleness may not apply to each situation in the same degree. We may have to seek a different balance between creating safe space, protecting, and nurturing for each instance we need to use it.

The stories of Jesus protecting the poor against the religious leaders or zealots pose some good images for gentleness and the conflict that goes on around it. He is kneeing the Pharisees to protect the weak. Jesus is telling us about gentleness. He is teaching us about protective space. He is modeling nurturance. Jesus tells us about poor, lowly, sick, and desperate people that need to find safe space to seek God from within. He is leading us into an understanding of the need for gentle places in our lives and in our hearts.

In many ways, when I reiterate these words in my head as I write them—as they ruminate in me in the telling—I hear these words saying that the definition of CHURCH is the gentle space created with an eye toward protection and nurturance. It is also the definition of our hearts as well. Church and the heart are about this gentleness of Jesus. I am not sure that we are living out that reality in either the church or our hearts today.

Taking on the extra precautions required to be gentle around any fragile situation is not only time consuming, but energy consuming as well. It can wear you out to function on high-alert and hyper-sensitivity to threats and danger. Being in protection mode is tiresome. Imagine how exhausting it would be to be gentle in all situations.

The Fathers' of the Church had a term for the type of high-alert mode that it took to be in a state of constant gentleness. They called it "nepsis" or "watchfulness". It is the alertness required to live a genuine and integrated spiritual life. In reality the whole of the spiritual life requires this hyper-awareness. Not just gentleness. To be truly spiritual and fully spiritual, one must increase the level of alertness and awareness one has in life. This is a tough proposition, to say the least.

This kind of awareness is what Jesus was getting at in the story of the wise and foolish virgins. We must be paying attention to all that is going on around us and processing it in order to know how to respond in the deepest and fullest way we are able—appropriate to each situation. The watchful virgins were keeping ready for the return of the bridegroom. They were protecting their lamps for the procession. It takes that same deep-alertness to be gentle with people and situations in your life.

Some schools work on teaching children the all pervasive nature of parenting and the nurturing protection that goes along with this role in life by having them carry around an egg with them all day. The children must keep an uncooked egg—in its shell—with them at all times throughout the day (some for several days on end). The aim is to teach the students about the fragile nature of an infant, to help them register the focus required to tend another living being, and to help them take some responsibility for one specific thing over an extended period of time—something that is fragile.

The exercise is a good one, not just in imparting the extensive amount of energy required to be a caregiver, but it also lets people know that it requires and extensive amount of energy just to be alert and watchful in general. Taking care of an egg is probably as difficult as taking care of a heart; or, of a church for that matter.

How watchful are you in life? Do you notice when other people are in need of nurturance and protection? Are you able to turn the perception of needed nurturance into an ability to nurture?

> *Leaders keep the people in their care safe. Their awareness of what is going on enables them to respond with a fashioned gentleness that exudes safety, protection, and nurturance.*

Connectivity Toolbox
—Stuff for your Journal

- Write in your journal about one instance when you can remember Jesus not being gentle with the people that were in the Temple.
- Write about why He was not being gentle. What had these people done?
- Did His act protect any other group of people? Who? How? Write this out in your journal.
- Take an uncooked egg and keep it with you for a day. Wherever you go, make sure the egg goes with you. Whatever you do you need to make provisions for keeping the egg safe and unbroken.
- Write about this experience in your journal? Was it hard?
- What does it mean to be watchful? Think about it for a few days and then jot down some ideas that come to mind—in your journal.
- List some examples (in your journal) of people being gentle with you through the years.
- Who is the gentlest person you know? How have they been gentle with other people?
- What animal and what color come to mind when you think of the trait of gentleness? Write them in your journal with a few sentences on why they come to mind for you when you think of gentleness.
- Workbook pages at: http://feedmysheepleadmysheep.blogspot.com/

9

Self-Control

SELF-CONTROL IS THE ABILITY to form and direct your immediate environment within (emotions, thoughts, desires) and without (actions and words) in order to obtain something that you value as a prize or a reward at a later time. It is a self-regulating or self-managing skill based on future pay offs. It is the control of the self (small "s" which connects it to the ego and all of its apparatus and manifestations). In our faith, we exert self-control over certain interior and exterior activities because Jesus has asked us to act a certain way in our relationship with Him and with all of His creation.

We seek to control our activities so we may live more like Jesus. We seek to control our activities so we may draw closer to Him. This drawing closer to Him and living like Him is also played out in our belief that we will be able to spend eternity with Him if we do as He asks. Another way of saying all this—without having to drag ourselves through the plethora of denominational and faith based expositions on what it means to be "saved" or "born-again"—would be to say, as Jesus did, "If you love me you will obey what I command" (Gospel of Saint John, xiv, 15). We seek to control our lives so that we may fulfill the commands of our Sweetest LORD, Jesus.

Far from being a simple exercise in mental clamping down and dogged will power, scientists are finding that we may be affecting our ability to control ourselves in the diets we espouse and the amount of downtime and rest we allow ourselves to participate in. The simple fact that we are having a hard time with self-control in more than one area of our lives may be a sign that we are over-exerting ourselves and diminishing our inner reserves of will-power. Our inabilities in the spiritual life may be more about how little balanced nutrition and rest we are allowing ourselves to partake of and less about how much we love God and long to obey Him. We may be hindering our own ability to have self-regulating and self-managing behavior in our lives.

When the fuel indicator needle in a car is on "E" we do not expect that we will be able to take that car on a vacation unless we "fill the tank". Why, when we are exhausted, over-extended, and living beyond our means and capabilities do we expect that we can do more and more and more by simply taking on more and more and more.

Part of the reason we are losing our ability to self-regulate is attached to not realizing we are running on a limited supply of energy; and also on not exerting a sense of honoring of that limit by saying "no". If we would realize will-power is a limited commodity—fueled by our nutrition and rest—we may be able to exert it with more accuracy and success. This requires learning to say "no" as well.

A simple assessment of how much we are doing can be helpful. Asking ourselves if we feel overtired may also help. If we notice that we are going on and on and on with lists of activities, we may need to tell ourselves that we have clearly lost control and are doing too much. We may also have to go back through the list and say "no" to a few things, so we can survive the life we are choosing to live.

I think most of us know that we are all too driven toward activity and that a lot of what we do has little or no significance in our journey other than fulfilling our need to have obligations and activities. Look at how much we sign up for just so we can tell ourselves that we are giving our kids a good childhood. Really? That is what we think we are doing?

Two of the nutrients that we would do well to incorporate into our lives are not foods in the common sense of the word; and yet, without these we would starve and die—or, at least, get extremely sick. We need stillness and silence in our lives. We need them in our lives every day.

The spiritual directors of many faith-based Christian contemplative movements have suggested twenty minutes in the morning and twenty minutes in the evening. We need this time to just sit and be still and silent. Building this sort of rest into our lives could help us to become more balanced from an interior perspective. It could give us the space we need to say "no" to things that clutter our lives and make us sickly. It could give us the space we need to say "yes" to surrendering more and more of our heart to Jesus.

Whether we take on a formal meditation practice or "centering prayer" practice, or just sit and ruminate on one verse of scripture or one thought centering on Jesus, will be up to us as individuals. What is essential is that we build this time into our lives.

This is not journaling time (although this is a helpful practice that may accompany your stillness); it is time to simply "be" with God. If simply sitting in stillness and silence unnerves us—as it tends to at first—I would suggest we look into the works of Thomas Keating, OCSO, Basil Pennington, OCSO, or Richard Rohr, OFM. All of these spiritual directors offer some "form" or "practice" of interior prayer to inhabit our contemplative time with. These "forms" provide formation and direction to our life. Eventually, when we have rehearsed and exercised the wings of our contemplative heart, we will be able to soar without the devices we need at the beginning.

I think about how I act when I am sick. I am grouchy, crabby, and more inclined to compromise my beliefs and do things I do not agree with when I am not feeling well. That same sort of dis-ease that comes from being sick is really the same thing I feel in my life when I am over worked, stressed to the max, and not taking care of my intake of nutrients and rest. Something has got to give. It is worth spending some time with Jesus to get that perspective back again.

Leaders recognize that without stillness and silence in their lives, they will have very little access to self-control on a deeper more mature level.

Connectivity Toolbox
—Stuff for your Journal

- List in your journal the main areas that you have trouble in controlling yourself. They might include: judging others, eating, lusting, coveting wealth.

- Under each of the areas you listed in your journal for the above toolbox bullet, list several concrete examples of ways you have lost the ability to control your immediate environment to obtain a greater good. For example, under judging others you may list: I am harsh in judging my children, I spend too much time picking apart what the pastor does, or I care too much about how much money other people make.

- Keep a list in your journal—for one week—of all of the foods, drinks, and snacks you eat throughout the course of the day. Be sure to list the times you eat and drink these items.

- Look back over the above list in your journal and see if you can identify any recurring gaps in your intake or any other repeated or cyclic occurrences in regard to your intake. Could these cycles be connected to shifts in blood sugar and consequently will power?

- Take a look at the works of Thomas Keating, OCSO, Basil Pennington, OCSO, and Richard Rohr, OFM on-line. See if you can research some of the simple daily practices they suggest for creating interior space. Journal about what you find.

- Take a look at "Centering Prayer" through Googling the words. How does it differ from "Welcoming Prayer"? Which of these would you like to try for a week? Journal about your experiences with these forms of interior prayer over the course of the week.

- In your journal, make a list of all the activities you are currently involved in. List work, home, and church projects as well as things you are involved with for your spouse and children and extended family. Take an honest look at this list and ask Jesus if some of these things need to go—so you can build rest and nutrition into your life at a deeper level. What do you feel He was saying to you about this—write it out in your journal.

- Workbook pages at: http://feedmysheepleadmysheep.blogspot.com/

10

Poverty of Spirit

It is hard to wrap one's heart let alone one's mind around the idea of poverty of spirit. There are so many different takes on poverty of spirit that you could write tomes on the number of things that people have said about it. I think the piece of this idea that I want to latch onto in our short discussion here is that poverty of spirit is about recognizing the truth of our connectedness. We are all interconnected.

Poverty of spirit begins and ends—from where I sit—in the idea that we have nothing and or are nothing without our connections to the whole. This means our connection to family, friends, believers, creation, the universe, and the Trinity Itself. As a matter of fact, the Trinity becomes a tipping point in our understanding of the deep-seated nature of interdependence that courses through all creation and un-Created Being. Everything is inextricably woven together with strands of the each and every; interlacing throughout the rich fabric and tapestry of life. Even the fullness of the Godhead is woven within Itself throughout.

We do not stand alone as an island; an idea that John Donne and Thomas Merton succinctly put forth in their writings. Let me say it another way: poverty of spirit is a blazing honesty and transparency about where our worth comes from. Our worth comes from our connection to the whole not our own singular piece in that whole alone.

I want to go back to all of the other discussions on poverty of spirit that we have entertained over the years. I think that most of them delve into a self-emptying discussion. That is, we are meant to abase ourselves and lower our perceptions of ourselves. We are to humbly bow before the LORD, recognizing our place in things. I think that this is exactly what I am getting at above; only I have added a bit of a twist to it. We not only need to recognize our "unworthiness", we need to recognize this "unworthiness" as incompleteness. I am not whole without the Other/other. I am not complete without the whole.

Poverty of spirit does not need to be reminiscent of having a bout with clinical depression or having no self-esteem. If you read between the lines of some modern authors, this is exactly how the teachings and writings of the church have been interpreted. This is not the case. We are truly poor in spirit when we recognize we do not stand alone. We are connected to a greater whole, and in fact are dependent on the greater whole.

Jesus is part of that greater whole. So are the Father and the Holy Spirit. The church is a part of that greater whole—the living church and the church triumphant. All of the people of all time fit into that greater whole—in and out of our own faith groupings. The earth and all the universe is a part of that greater whole—from the smallest quark to the grandest quasar. You want to feel poverty of spirit in the center of your chest? Take a look at some Hubble Telescope images of "ultra deep space". I do not know how all the pieces of the greater whole fit together, but I know that it is bigger than me. FOR SURE!

This vastness of the cosmos and all that is, is really an unleashing of the depth of God and the expansiveness of Spirit. When we are talking about God, we are talking about an endlessness of Spirit that cannot be understood. We hold up the cosmos—or the matter of the universe—and it is nothing in comparison to the eternal nature of the Spirit that has created all that is.

When we see ourselves against the back drop of this Spirit, we see ourselves as poor. We are not poor because of some unreasonable shame. We are poor in shear comparison to the greatness of Spirit. We are nothing in comparison. Seeing this, our heart takes a humble and interior assent to the fact that we are nothing without all of the rest of it. We need the whole.

Another keen biblical image concerning our poverty of spirit is revealed in the stories of our creation. We are told that we are made out of the dust and dirt of the earth and that when we die we will fall apart and go back into that dust, physically. Then we are told that the LORD removed a rib from the first man, Adam, and created Eve out of that. Both of these biblical narratives are tales of one thing coming from another; one thing made out of another. They are stories of dependence and interdependence.

Aside from showing us a connectivity of one thing to another—our lives to the earth and to each other—they also reveal a paradigm that instructs us on perspective and place. The stories remind us that we are no better than each other and that we are no better than the earth. We are made from the dirt and we are the building blocks for each other. This keeps us from allowing our sense of elevation to expand beyond control. Telling these tales gives us a primal and group sense of our station in the cosmos.

This is not meant to demean us as humans and deny our capabilities. It is meant to help us stay connected and gain a common ground in our identity. As we know from the development of the biblical narrative, it is this very base and humble creature that God has endowed with the ability to espouse and be filled with His Spirit. It is this lowly and dependent place that God chooses to inhabit and fill with His Presence. Once we have allowed ourselves to see how empty and connected we truly are, then we are fertile soil for Divine Planting; then God can fill us with His Spirit. He lifts up the meek and the lowly.

A leader recognizes that poverty of spirit comes from seeing ourselves in the overall scheme of God's full and complete universe—not simply our little slice of it.

Connectivity Toolbox
—Stuff for your Journal

- Google "The Hubble Ultra Deep Field in 3D" and either view images, video, or read up on what has been discovered. Make sure you include postings from You Tube in your search as well.

- Journal about the information you found in the above Google search and You Tube. What does this say about who you are in relation to the whole?

- Write an essay about the complexity of a Trinity that can create a universe like this as seen in the images of the ultra deep field.

- Write a letter in your journal describing the vastness of the ultra deep field images to your child (if you do not have a child, pretend you do). Help them understand what they are seeing and how they—as a human—fit into the whole. Share this with your group.

- Look through a concordance for verses on the heavens. Read some and journal about what you find. Be sure to spend some time reading Job xxxviii, 1–33 and journaling about what is imagined in those passages.

- Open up your journal and review where you have been since the beginning of this Feed My Sheep; Lead My Sheep journey. What do you notice in your writing? Is there a sense of expanding thought or a deepening of ideas? What impresses you or catches your attention?

- Write down a list of some of the things you notice about yourself in the journal you have been keeping? Share these and discuss them with your group.

- Do something this week for another person simply because you are deeply connected and interwoven. Show them signs of support and connection. Let them know you value their connection.

- Workbook pages at: http://feedmysheepleadmysheep.blogspot.com/

11

Mourning

Mourning appears in our lives and is available to us at several levels. There is the need to feel a sense of sadness when we step out of a wholesome and more accurate understanding of who we are in the face of God and all of the cosmos; a sense of longing to be reunited with our "connected whole" when we recognize our departure from the Spirit of God.

There is also a need to weep and gnash our teeth when we feel a sense of separation from any of our connected wholeness—grieving the loss of the people and places in our lives because of circumstance. Mourning is looking at the fact that although we are deeply interconnected and woven within a common fabric of the Divine Creative Father, there are times we feel and notice separation. This separation opens us to the opportunity to mourn and be renewed.

People that are able to mourn and grieve tend to be pretty honest people. You have to be able to acknowledge a sense of separation at some level in order to mourn and grieve. People that pretend—all of the time—that everything is ok and they never feel a sense of separation are not being honest with themselves. They will not be able to mourn appropriately.

Sometimes, in our lives, we hold on so tightly to the illusion that we are doing fine and that we never feel separation from a larger whole-self and our Father that a small breakdown occurs and we are forced into momentary collapse and tears. We pick up the pieces and look around; making sure no one saw us. This is not mourning. Mourning comes from a deep acknowledgement that although we are deeply connected as people, there are moments when a tear in the fabric occurs and we cannot explain our sense of separation and we grieve that.

This deep acknowledgement of a tear in the fabric and the brokenness of that which is whole is a continuation of the perspective we noticed in seeing the cosmos and our place in it. Mourning is a connecting with the reality that even though we are a part of a larger whole—a part of God's family, the cosmos, the church, and a community—we experience moments of death and separation. This may be the death of dreams and situations in our lives or it may be the death of people in our lives. These deaths, when we feel them inside of ourselves—honestly, cause us to weep and mourn and grieve. We are turned to wishing and imagining that we could have back that which we lost.

It is at this place of raw and open vulnerability to the truth of separation and loss that exists in a unified cosmos that is the departure point for healing. From a place of connecting and cathecting with our losses in life—when we mourn openly—we are able to be comforted by God and other people. We have to get to the place of feeling the separation and loss of connectivity and then expressing it freely by mourning and weeping before we can truly be comforted back into wholeness and healing.

This type of scenario unfolds when we sin and feel separate from our Creative Father. It happens when we get divorced, lose our jobs, our children move off, our parents die, our friends abandon us. It also happens when we choose to separate ourselves from unhealthy habits and situations—things that are dangerous to our survival and growth.

This last scenario—the one of choosing to separate ourselves—is a highly advanced skill and a sign of maturity. It is also a loss that we engage with by our own choice. So many other losses in our lives we can say are out of our control. This choosing to cut ourselves off from something—healthy or unhealthy—is much more complex as we ultimately carry not only the loss with us, but a sense of blame or responsibility for the separation. Fasting is just such an activity. In fasting we choose to separate ourselves from something (a good or bad habit) in order to gain perspective. These self imposed losses are examples of complicated grieving and loss. There are others, but this is clearly one example. It makes the edges of our understanding of what is going on in our grief a little hazy or fuzzy. We are less able to identify all the features of what we are feeling.

Any one of these shifts—if viewed with honesty and poverty of spirit—would cause us to feel a tear in the unified weave of the fabric. Whether we allow ourselves to openly express our "undoneness" our "fallen-apartness" or our "brokenness" at the loss, is up to us. But, it is critical in healing back into wholeness that we are able to openly connect with this loss and then mourn as a result.

Taking a look at mourning and weeping in the spiritual development of the Christian community over time adds a powerful and rich overlay of meaning to this simple statement of Jesus in the Beatitudes. In the early desert movement in Christianity and up to the present (mostly, but not exclusively in the development of spirituality in the Christian East—the Byzantine and Oriental forms) a whole pathos evolved around "tears" in the life of the believer.

Many of the Fathers and Mothers of the desert had a sense of "weeping bitterly over their sins" that morphed into a whole lifestyle. They perceived and imagined the gaps and separations that exist between God and humanity. They felt deeply the suffering that emerges from those gaps. They learned to imitate and embody the "groaning of all creation" for a day when things would be made whole. They walked around weeping continuously for the separation we all feel. As a result a whole vocation emerged of individuals who became not only a reminder to us of the gaps in the fabric, but showed us how to reconnect with our "cataracts within" and unleash the tears of mourning. They were reminders that weeping is part of getting back to the place of wholeness. And, at some point in coming to terms with the disparities in life, the tears of mourning are turned into the tears of consolation. We experience—in our mourning—a healing and a rich understanding of the beauty, complexity, and awesomeness of life. Those who had the "gift of tears" wept for all of this and beckon us to do the same.

People that never connect with this angst and suffering of separation and loss (as well as the rich understanding of the beauty, complexity, and awesomeness of life) are really out of touch and not moving toward wholeness. In many ways they are unrealistic and unhealthy.

Leaders are not afraid to show that they understand the beauty of the cosmos and our wholesome relation to God; and, at the same time that there are profound gaps and separations in life that demand we mourn deeply and openly.

Connectivity Toolbox
—*Stuff for your Journal*

- Journal about the times in your life you have mourned and wept openly. Make sure you include a discussion about what "separation" or "loss" it was that you were feeling.

- Google the term "the gift of tears" and journal about what you find.

- Copy this quote of Saint Isaac of Nineveh in your journal: *"The heart that is inflamed in this way embraces the entire creation—man, birds, animals and even demons. At the recollection of them, and at the sight of them, such a man's eyes fill with tears that arise from the great compassion which presses on his heart. The heart grows tender and cannot endure to hear of or look upon any injury or even the smallest suffering inflicted upon anything in creation. For this reason such a man prays increasingly with tears even for irrational animals and for the enemies of truth and for all who harm it, that they may be guarded and be forgiven. The compassion which pours out from his heart without measure, like God's, extends even to reptiles."*

- Write about what this quote means in your journal. Share that with your group.

- Journal about why it is that we may be moved to mourning because we have a richer understanding of the beauty, complexity, and awesomeness of life. What could move us to have this kind of understanding?

- Find someone in your life that is mourning and grieving and reach out to them and let them know you are there. Nothing more. Simply let them know you see their hurt and that you are connected to them and love them.

- Read this article http://tjm-griefarticles.posterous.com/giving-voice and journal about the path of grief and mourning in our lives.

- Workbook pages at: http://feedmysheepleadmysheep.blogspot.com/

12

Meekness

MEEKNESS IS ONE OF those character traits that have been given a bum rap. Like poverty of spirit, meekness tends to get played off as some form of clinical depression or diminished self-esteem. It is often seen as fearful timidity. This is not the point of meekness, nor is it the core of this characteristic. That is a form of illness masquerading as a positive attribute; anxiety posing as humility.

Meekness (like poverty of spirit) is a feeling of humility in the heart. But, meekness expresses itself (moves outside of the heart and the simply feeling) with the help of self-control by creating space for "the other". It is making room for another to shine—rather than oneself. Meekness is a pulling back of your own ego (humility) in such a way as to make the other (God, person, situation, etc.) more important or central to what is going on at the moment. Meekness is posturing yourself as a signpost for someone or something else: pointing the way.

There is a wonderful image of the Virgin and Child in which Mary gestures toward her Son. She is indicating the Way. The icon is called "The Indicator of the Way" ("Hodigetria" in Greek). It is a classic visual on what meekness is all about. One soul bows out of the way in order for another to be seen. It is an unveiling or uncovering of something/someone more important. You get this same image in Saint John the Forerunner's words about himself when he says, "He must become greater; I must become less" (Gospel of Saint John iii, 30). He is talking about Jesus in this passage. These two central images of meekness really drive it home as a core value of the follower of Jesus.

Leaders are able to help replicate this value in followers of Jesus—The Way. They role model this quintessential reenactment of Gospel teaching. The leader must indicate the way, like the Virgin Mary. The leader must also allow Jesus to become greater, so their importance becomes less.

This means facilitating the ability of the individuals around you and instigating their desires. You have to fuel the fires and step back allowing people a chance to do some of the work on their own. You have to rely on that "crest jewel"—discrimination—to learn the dance of meekness. When do I approach with ample space to allow this person to shine? When do I step in and offer some support or direction so they may shine all the more? Meekness is not timidity, but it is not only making space for others. It is engaging those others in growth-full opportunity in that created space.

Meekness is not apathy in the lazy sense of the word. A lot of people in church leadership could stake claims on meekness in the ground of laziness. They have not one cell of "drive" in their body. This should not be confused with being meek. Meekness is calculated. You have to watch for the moments in which you will create the space for another to shine. You cannot simply punctuate life with space anywhere and at any time. You must orchestrate the establishment of space. You must coax the individual out and get them to shine.

It would be fair to say that a lot of meekness is the same as playing second fiddle. As a leader, however, it is a chosen role because you are trying to accentuate the work of the other fiddle player. It is also part and parcel of playing second fiddle that you will—in this case—step up and offer instruction to the first fiddle that will enhance their skill and chance to expose it. We do a lot of this by helping followers of Jesus learn how to lead other people either to Christ, or in some organizational capacity.

The points that are critical to overhear are these: meekness is intentionally creating the space for another and it is attached to the responsibility of giving feedback or some sort of closure communication to the one you have created space for—or the group. It is a part of the formation and direction process.

Let us just say that a member of your small group comes home from a mission trip. You can create the space for them by speaking to the group about the great job that this person did in going to such and such a place and doing such and such a thing. Ask them to speak about it for a little. Ask them leading questions to draw them out and detail the work. When they are finished, wrap it up by thanking them for doing this wonderful thing in the name of Jesus. Tell them you are proud and that their ability to humble themselves and serve has left a valuable impact on someone else's life.

Or, you allow your violin student to perform a solo for a group of friends. You create the space for them to do it. After they have finished you draw attention to the wonderful performance and you speak to the student privately as well—extolling the virtues of the performance and offering pointers as needed. Intentionally create space; but accentuate what has been displayed or revealed in that space. It is a full circle. Anything less is really just lack of planning and avoidance. Too often we say that people who fail to engage or plan are meek. This is not the case.

When this pattern of creating space for others is evolved in a group, the leader actually can practice a fuller sense of meekness. They can just introduce the notion or idea and the follower of Jesus will have been formed enough as a leader that they will automatically fulfill the other functions mentioned in the process. The leader is being intentional and the follower of Jesus is taking on the responsibility aspect of meekness.

There are deeper forms of meekness. Creating silence in a group is a deep form of meekness. It is stepping back to allow some interior work to be done. This is vital. But, as stated above, it is intentional and is best to describe the process to the group as a way of becoming meek as a group. You could tell the group that, "We will observe some silence in order for us to reflect or meditate as individuals. We are going to practice meekness as a group; creating a space for us to hear the Spirit's call in our heart."

As leaders, we are also called to be meek before God. We model this. We approach God with humility. We allow God the space to speak to us. We listen and then we respond by telling God what we have heard Him say when we are through.

> *Leaders create a space for others to be revealed in; for others to shine in. They also take responsibility for actively reflecting back to people what they have seen happen in that space; offering instruction as needed.*

Connectivity Toolbox
—Stuff for your Journal

- Why would Jesus say that the meek would inherit the earth? Why would this be an appropriate inheritance for the meek? Write about this in your journal. Share this with your group.

- Plan a whole meeting that will allow you to practice meekness for others in the group. It may be your family; it may be a class or simply a gathering of some friends. Do not make it into a stage production, but clearly make space for others to shine, draw them out and reflect back what has been revealed. Write about how it went in your journal.

- Or, plan a whole meeting that will allow your whole group (the one doing this study) to practice meekness as a group. Practice helping to create space for others to shine—in the group. Draw out their conversation and comments. Reflect back some encouraging/helpful statements. Discuss the process and how it went as a group when you are finished.

- Write in your journal about the above experience. How did you feel watching other people shine and open up? How do you feel being given the opportunity to shine for others?

- Meekness is often seen as a cure for pride, arrogance, and haughtiness. How can being meek help with these three sinful attitudes? Journal about this and discuss this as a group.

- List five leaders in your journal who never create space for others. How toxic is their presence? Do people really grow around them? Or do people simply adore them?

- Copy Izaak Walton's quote in your journal—*"God has two dwellings: one in heaven, and the other in a meek and thankful heart"*

- Journal about what you think Izaak Walton was getting at in this quote.

- Workbook pages at: http://feedmysheepleadmysheep.blogspot.com/

13

Hungering and Thirsting for Righteousness

IF THERE IS ANYTHING that the process of aging does for us is that it helps us come to terms with being honest with ourselves and recognizing who we really are. This is not a by-product of getting older; it is a by-product of taking a long hard look at our life over and over again—all through our life. The advantage of age is that we have done this more often and should be learning the lessons in a deeper sense because of the repetition of processing our patterns. With this discriminatory process comes the understanding of the truth that we are always hungry for something. We are always thirsty for something. We always crave and desire something.

The hunger is always present. It is our biological urge to grow and survive into the future. It is cellular and not something we can turn on and off. The hunger persists. The body has this hunger, but so too does the mind, and the heart, and the soul as well. They are all a means of swelling our lives into tomorrow. Every area of our lives is hungry. What will we allow them to be hungry for? We chose the object of our desiring; not that we desire. To not choose the object of our desiring could set our default longings with settings we do not feel comfortable with nor condone.

Many will disagree on this point because they will be impressed with the notion that this is a hedonist idea. Not so. How we choose to direct the hunger in us will determine whether we are hedonists or not. We can move the hunger into righteous categories and that will make all the difference—as Robert Frost said.

The idea of righteousness and the righteous man were powerfully alive during Jesus' lifetime and the whole inter-testamental time period in general. The Qumran find of the Dead Sea Scrolls contained numerous texts that spoke of one called the "Teacher of Righteousness". It was the longing of the people that the Messiah, or this Righteous Teacher would appear and set them free. Of course, everyone then, as now, had their own idea of just what it meant for this Teacher to set them free.

The driving force behind a righteous man is that he is trying to set "all things right". It is an all pervasive kind of "righting of the wrong". It is "rightness" at all levels in life. If the righteous man errs, he simply repents and enters back into setting things right. This stands in contradistinction to the notion of the "just man".

The just man is the man who does a little more "good" than he does "bad". He may be fifty-one percent good, but that is all it takes to be just. He must always strive to balance the accounts a bit more in the favor of the good so he is justified.

A righteous man is on a quest to get it all right—inside him and all around him. It is a quest for the whole of creation, not his soul alone. And, he falls and gets up with the drive to return to his path—selling all he has to obtain the goal, not just a little more than what it takes.

The Talmud teaches that there are 36 righteous men/women on the earth at any given time. Without them longing to set this whole creation right, the earth and the universe itself would topple into the abyss. Without this hungering and thirsting for "making all things new"— making them right—there would be no sustainability for creation. The reality is that all of creation leans into hungering and thirsting for more and more; it is simply a matter of what it sets itself to hunger and thirst for that is critical. The righteous man/woman chooses the right.

The Fathers and Mothers of the Church and the Rabbis of the Synagogue were constantly arguing about the power and place of imagination in the life of the believer. Imagination drove many a heated debate in the early days of formation and direction in developing the theological and philosophical teachings of both Christianity and Judaism. Today, these conversations are lost to our ears. In reality, the issues that drove these conversations are equally as prevalent and in need of discussion— we just do not notice. We are blown all over the seas of our hearts and minds and souls by the winds of desire and imagining. We just do not talk about it much.

The things that we put before our eyes—and the rest of the senses as well—will take root in us as we water their seeds with ongoing participation. If we see billboards over and over again with trim and sleek bodies consuming the "finer things in life" we will eventually be watering the seeds of "trim and sleek bodies" in our lives and we will—at some level—begin to yearn for and long for their presence in our lives. Even if we do not "lust" after this, we will at least make these images into "the ideal" and we will hunger and thirst to become "like" them as we grow into our lives.

What we place or allow in the spaces all around us will inform our body's, heart's, mind's, and soul's desires. What we give assent to in our physical spaces will eventually take up housing in our imagination and interior spaces.

What will you long for and crave? What will you allow to fill your heart, mind, soul, and body? How will you allow your imagination and growth toward tomorrow to hunger and thirst?

> *A leader knows that the desiring nature is part of what it means to grow. They learn to direct the focus of their longing toward the right and wholesome things in life.*

Connectivity Toolbox
—*Stuff for your Journal*

- In your journal list out ten things you currently desire with and for your body? What could you replace them with if you find that some of them are not healthy? List those next to the original desire.

- In your journal list out ten things you currently desire with and for your mind? What could you replace them with if you find that some of them are not healthy? List those next to the original desire.

- Do the same for your heart and soul as well.

- Copy this quote in your journal: *"Whom have I in heaven but you? And earth has nothing I desire besides you."*—Psalm lxxiii, 25.

- Draw a picture or write a poem in your journal about the quote above.

- Keep a running list—throughout a day or two—of all the things you see in the media and the advertising around you that are planting themselves in you as seeds of desiring. Write about how they impact your worldview and imagination.

- Copy this quote from Epicurus in your journal: *"Not what we have, but what we enjoy, constitutes our abundance."*

- Journal about what the above quote means to you.

- Talk with your group about the kinds of things you all think you should be longing and desiring for if you are to become righteous and move the whole of creation toward righteousness.

- Workbook pages at: http://feedmysheepleadmysheep.blogspot.com/

14

Mercifulness

The "Legends of the Jews" edited by Louis Ginzberg is a wonderful collection of tales of midrashic detail and oral tradition. The volumes go through Hebraic salvation history and lay out the "behind the scenes" stories that the scriptural canon omits. Many people say the stories are made up of the remnants of deep mythological content from their telling and retelling among the tribes and around the fires—outside of formal and structural faith and religion. They are wonderful reading.

In the tales that emerge around the life of Adam and Eve there is revealing story about Adam's death. Adam lies dying at the ripe old age of 930. He calls to his son, Seth, and asks him to return to the Garden of Eden and beg the Archangel Michael for oil from the tree of mercy. Adam knows it will soothe his pain and anguish as he waits for death.

Seth goes to the Garden and begs. The Archangel Michael tells Seth that Adam is not permitted to receive this gift until him (Adam) and all the chosen are reunited in Paradise. All mankind will receive the anointing of this healing balm at that time. Adam must die with a sense of travail, but with the hope of final restoration and unending mercy in the Garden yet to come.

I love how this story weaves a sense of yearning and disappointment into an understanding of suffering and then ultimate redemption. The story lets us know that all of our ailments will be anointed with the oil of the tree of mercy in the life to come. And, at that time God will set us free with His own healing balm.

Mercy is like that. It is a healing balm that we yearn for. When we are anointed with mercy, we are calmed and settled into restoration of body and soul (mind and heart as well). Mercy is the healing of things that ail us; a being made to feel whole once again.

With this kind of definition of mercy it is not hard to come up with instances of mercy in life. The first and most natural place to begin to look for these examples of mercy would be in cases of tender restoration and healing of others: helping a child who has skinned their knee, visiting the sick and dying in their homes or hospitals, and offering a cool drink of water to those parched with thirst. The very journey of Seth to beg for mercy is a solace and form of mercy for Adam.

The thing that accompanies mercy that makes such an immense and marked impact is the sense of relief that emerges. Everything is building up and heading in one direction; the sick are getting sicker, the thirsty cannot slake their thirst. And then, some act of relief comes in and calms down the need that is building to out of control proportions. A doctor brings healing to the sick and a friend brings water to the thirsty. The need is met and things can settle down again.

We have all had the chance to participate in an act of mercy that brings this kind of release to the soul of another. We have also been able—all of us—to receive some act of mercy that opens us up to feeling release ourselves. The whole thing is freeing.

Let me add a layer of history to the midrashic tales of Adam on his sick bed. In the pseudepigraphal Gospel of Nicodemos—a gospel heavily quoted and alluded to in Anglo-Saxon Christianity—the same story is told with a slight deviation. In the gospel book Seth is asked to look into the Garden through its gate. When he does, has a vision that the Archangel must interpret. Seth sees a young child in the Garden among the trees. Michael tells him that this Child is the Son of God and it is He that is the Oil of Mercy. It is the Child that shall restore fallen Adam. He sends Seth back to his father with three grains and a whole list of things Seth must do (the classic hero's journey stuff). The point of the story is that the Early Church knew of the tales concerning the attempt to bring healing to the dying Adam and they helped to reinterpret the tales of the Synagogue for the early Christian believers. Christ Himself is the Oil of Mercy.

This being the case it is clear that the Early Church teaching on mercy is equal to that of the teaching on atonement and redemption. What Christ did to bring us all into paradise is the meaning of mercy. We are tired and burned out from trying to do things on our own; mercy sets us free. We are exasperated at trying again and again to do things without sinning; mercy sets us free. We want so desperately to do the things we know we should, but can only do the things we know we should not do; mercy sets us free.

Mercy is about offering relief to people when all they are doing is spinning their wheels. Finding ways to take away the suffering of repeated failure and constant need is one way to provide mercy. This is why we see the acts of mercy as feeding the hungry, clothing the naked, visiting the sick and imprisoned. The life of the hungry is a constant state of hunger. Bringing them food brings them relief. The life of the imprisoned is a constant state of isolation. Visiting them brings them relief.

The mercy that Christ offers is longer lasting than what we can give. He gives a restoration for all eternity. We simply bring a restoration for a short time—a small dose. But, the relief we bring in acts of mercy is a foreshadowing and an echo of the full-blown mercy of Jesus. Our acts of restoration mirror the complete work that Jesus can do for people.

A leader knows when people are worn out—he hears their cry for relief. A leader turns to them in their hour of need and fills them with the good things they lack.

Connectivity Toolbox
—Stuff for your Journal

- In your journal, write about one time when you were able to offer mercy to someone that was in distress. How did this make you feel? What was the impact of the act of mercy? How did the other person feel?

- In your journal, write about one time when you were able to receive mercy from someone else while you were in distress. How did this make you feel? What was the impact of the act of mercy? How did the other person feel?

- Make a list of five people in your life that are in some form of distress (in your journal). List the distress next to the name.

- Find one way to offer "the oil of mercy" to each of the five people on your list. Write in your journal about the experience of helping to restore them to "health" and "release" them from their ailment. Do this for each of the five experiences.

- Draw a picture or write a poem about "mercy" in your journal.

- What color would mercy be? Share this in your group; along with your reason why.

- Google "acts of mercy" or "works of mercy" and write about (in your journal) what the acts of mercy/works of mercy are and how you can fulfill them in the lives of those in need.

- Write about (in your journal) whether or not the "state" or the "government" should be responsible for acts of mercy / works of mercy and programs to support the welfare of its member or whether people of faith should be responsible to do this and leave it out of the hands of government and the state.

- Workbook pages at: http://feedmysheepleadmysheep.blogspot.com/

15

Purity of Heart

THE PROCESS OF MAKING something pure requires refinement. In the process of making precious metals pure; removing any dross that floats to the surface requires heating the metal until it is molten. In this case the refinement process involves massive heat. It is really not much different in the purification of the heart—massive amounts of refining energy are applied to our lives. Sometimes this energy feels like heat, sometimes like pressure, and perhaps even sometimes like a deep freeze. Regardless the form the energy takes, it is these trials or sufferings in life—adverse conflicts or seemingly athletic tests—that strengthen us, refine us, and add layers of character almost like scar tissue.

I think we often have an idyllic image of what purity of heart looks like in someone. Usually we imagine they are a straight-laced character. We assume a pure hearted person is unfamiliar with the idea or reality of sin; someone who has never sinned and or would not even think of sinning. This does not bear up under scrutiny when we consider what it is that makes someone pure. Purity of heart may be present in the innocent and ignorant; people who have never been in a situation that requires them to make a choice between right and wrong—sort of as a "virgin" or "original" state of reality. But, it is not present there by choice, but by default. They do not know another way.

True purity of heart is seen in people who know full well the good and bad of a situation and battle within themselves to choose the good. Its true worth is found in the one who chooses to be pure amid the desirous pull to live in pleasure alone. It is choosing one's way even when massive conflict must be endured to emerge from that way. We rail against Adam and Eve for "falling" in the Garden, but without that fall they would have remained unrefined creatures.

Purity of Heart   63

Rather than producing some translucent waif-like characters and two dimensional saints, purity of heart in its most mature showing produces wild-men and wild-women like Saint John the Forerunner, Elijah, and Saint Mary of Egypt. The timid wispiness we equate with piety and sanctity is not only useless, but a just plain deflated understanding of holiness. The pure of heart are people with an erect spine—men and women with a backbone. They face into the wind; they do not flee from it.

The tawdry and weak saints (the mild and timid ones) could never stand up against the wiles of the Adversary, let alone the un-Christ-like behavior that appears present in the local church from time to time. It takes vim, vigor, and guts to be pure in heart. It takes battle and battle-scars to mature in an understanding of clarity of purpose. After all, what else is purification if it is not clarifying our vision and righteous action itself?

As in other virtues, this is not about timidity. That image of "the timid" should be struck from the annals of our understanding of sanctity. There can be no element of timidity in the saints of God. It takes thunder in the heart to live, approach, and lead for the living God. The timid are like chaff, blown away at the least show of wind.

We spend a lot of our time on this earth trying to figure out whether or not the refinement process is sent by God. The whole Job-syndrome really rattles us and consumes our days. I think, in many ways, trying to decide whether the conflicts in life are sent by God or not is really a coping mechanism that is trying to figure out what is happening. It is an attempt to put some distance between us and the conflict—some space by which we can gain stability.

There is nothing wrong with this natural reaction to conflict. It is a knee jerk reaction that is a part of the process. How long we wander around in this state of "trying to assign blame"; however, is within our control. At some point in the discussion, we really need to back off trying to assign origin and blame and we need to get into the heart of the matter and grow into surviving through the conflict with as much integrity and character as we can. Too often people stop with the assigning of origin and blame. When we do this, we never deepen.

We have all met people who have stopped here. They leave a sort of nasty taste in our mouth or a sense of shallowness in our heart. Some calamity befalls them and they say things like. "It is God's will." Or, "God is trying to make me stronger." I am not arguing for or against God's place in our trials. I feel it is an unanswerable dilemma. I am arguing for deepening our lives and purifying our hearts in and through the process of conflicts in our lives.

This is what happens to Job in the end. He has this massive dialogue with God in which God lays out all of the mysteries of the universe. Job is reminded of his own poverty of spirit in view of the cosmos, and the story wraps up; Job beginning his life anew. Job tries to live with as much integrity as he is able to, given what has happened to him in the disasters of his days.

So, what is the take away? What does it mean to live through the conflict and become purified? I see that as what we wrestle with when we are in the midst of the suffering. What we should be arguing with—in our center—is how can I remain loving even though this is happening to me? How can I find peace in this craziness? How can I be righteous when I feel so weak? Purity of heart is about wrestling and struggling to be righteous in the midst of conflict. It is about trying to make right choices (not figure out why this is happening to me) in the thick of battle.

When someone emerges on the other side of the conflict, they are stronger, bloodier, and ready for rest. Purity of heart is about a whirlwind of activity and us trying to make it through. When it is over, we take stock of what we have lost, where we have been, and the new muscles we may have developed.

> *A leader knows that purity of heart is battling through conflict with a commitment to righteousness. They understand that it is a refining process.*

Connectivity Toolbox
—Stuff for your Journal

- In your journal, list five trials or ordeals you have been through in your life that feel to you like they were a refining process.
- Write about (in your journal) how it was going through these times of refinement and purification. What did you do to get through them? What have you put in to practice in your life as a result of what you learned during those trials?
- Google "refining gold" and read up on how the process occurs and what it entails. Write a rough outline of the process in your journal.
- Write (in your journal) about how the process of refining gold is similar to refining and purifying your heart.
- Google "Saint Mary of Egypt" and read up on her life? Journal about what you found to be interesting in her conversion. How does her life reveal the refinement process we are all a part of? What caused her to attain purity of heart?
- List all of the critical junctures in our lives that put us to the test (in your journal). Not just one or two. Try to come up with a comprehensive list of all the critical junctures you can think of. Share these lists with each other as a group. See if you can list the fruits that are produced as a result of living through these refining times of life. List them directly next to the critical juncture they apply to—in your journal.
- Pray for five people you know that are currently going through a refining process. Send them a note to let them know you prayed for them.
- Workbook pages at: http://feedmysheepleadmysheep.blogspot.com/

16

Peacemaker-Ship

BEING A PEACEMAKER GOES beyond the simple ability of finding peace in life and learning to relish and thrive in that peace. It is the ability to take what you have created in your own existence—with God's help—and enable others to see the value in it and facilitate their entrance into the process of building peace into their own lives. This can be enabling or facilitating peace in the lives of individuals and or groups. It is helping others plant a garden of peace.

We often think of it as helping individuals who are in a conflict with each other. Bringing peace to a relationship that is currently under stress; and it may well be that. It can also be helping groups of people learn to build space into their lives for meditation. It could be helping unwed mothers find time to get away from their children and devote time to their own soul and their own growth. The peace we are teaching and helping people to make is that spaciousness that gives us pause to stop defending ourselves and to simply be.

Remember what we discussed earlier concerning "peace" itself. It is a word that connotes and denotes wholeness, completeness, rest, and tranquility of soul. It reaches beyond our political sense of peace, which is often nothing more than the absence of chaos, conflict, or strife. It delves into the idea that we can actively restrain or limit things in our lives that lead to disturbances and the ruffling of tranquility in order to attain to a sense of calm. Peace is something we struggle to attain, not simply something that happens in the absence of war.

The peacemaker, then, is someone who is able to go beyond finding this peace within their own life and is able to help people (individuals and groups) "buy-into" the need for this type of peace and then "set-out" to attain this type of peace for themselves. It is the ability to set others on the path toward direction and formation. This makes it a complex-trait. Any trait that you must first attain to in your own life and then later try to inculcate in others is a complex-trait. It requires self-attainment and a certain degree of self-management in that attainment as well as the ability to clarify and impart the ability to attain it to others. Leadership is a series of one complex-trait after another.

While we are talking about the complex nature of traits that are planted in the life of another, we should mention a word about perfection here. No leader is perfect. No leader will ever be perfect. And yet, when we are hurt by people—leaders in particular—one of the first layers we end up having to peel back is the layer of shock that we feel. We are shocked that leaders sin.

Leaders need to be more transparent and confess when they are wrong; and confess that they are wrong often. It needs to be built into the dialogue of how we talk about life. We are ALL in this same condition together and that should be very evident in the language and the posturing that a leader takes.

Be aware of how you are setting yourself up to be perceived. If you have the heart of a leader, you best be sure that you are building poverty of spirit into how you talk about yourself to those you lead. Let them know that you do not have false pretenses of glory and perfection. There is no need to go overboard, but you do need to be open and honest.

The same is true with peacemaking. Make sure people know that you break the peace all the time. Tell people how you have been selfish in arguments with your spouse. Let them know that you have ruined your kids' day by yelling at them. Share that you sometimes seek your own sense of "winning" a dispute or church conflict. You and I alike destroy peaceful space when we enter into conflicts with others—so be honest with people. If you do not build confession into your leadership, you are building phony images of yourself and phony followers of Jesus.

What does peacemaker-ship look like in the world you inhabit? It can be helping families to spend some time together sharing their faith. It can be setting up a conflict resolution workshop for your small group—teaching them techniques for facilitating listening. It could be hosting a meeting of your men's group with a men's group at a homeless shelter in town.

However you seek to share the process of peacemaking with another individual or group it is all about creating a space for people to exist in with each other. The quality of this space should reflect an ability to listen to each other. It should also reflect the ability to be heard, to be taught, to be healed, to rest, to mend and to relax. People cannot find peace in the whole of their lives unless they have some small place they can go to practice peace. We need a small place in our lives where we can experience the depth of what peace feels like in our lives. Then we can yearn and learn to create it in other areas—even all areas—of our lives.

> *Peacemaker-ship is about setting up spaces and places where people can taste the experiences of wholeness and rest. Leaders are careful to build these kinds of spaces into the lives of the people they care for—making them hungry for more.*

Connectivity Toolbox
—Stuff for your Journal

- Write about (in your journal) how you resolve conflict. What do you do when someone hurts you? What about when they humiliate you? What about when they ignore you? How do you feel when you hurt others?
- Make a list in your journal of the most prominent people in history that have been peacemakers in your estimation.
- Write (in your journal) a few sentences about each of the peacemakers you listed above and what trait you think was/is central to their peacemaking. What was their message about peace? How did they deliver it?
- It is time to review your journal again. Start at the beginning and work your way through the whole of it. When you are finished, add a few lines to your journal about what you think you have noticed about your writing. Have you seen any growth? Do you feel like a different person from the person you were when you began this journey? Does your journal reveal some new pieces of yourself?
- Do a little research on conflict resolution. Take some notes on what you find. Discuss the things you find as a group and make up a joint list of skills and techniques that will help people to resolve conflict and plant a wholesomeness and peacefulness with others into their lives. Maybe you could even act on this information (as a group) and run a short session at church for other people on: *"resolving conflicts with each other".*
- Workbook pages at: http://feedmysheepleadmysheep.blogspot.com/

17

Persecuted for Righteousness

Taking on the challenge of planting and developing character traits in our lives is truly a massive effort. It is only one leg of the journey; however. It is one thing to build up strength in the heart and the mind toward being a better leader. It is quite another to do all of that while under fire from those who are trying to wound you.

Have no misunderstanding about where the attack will come from. It will most often be friendly-fire; shots will be taken at you by those in close proximity. If you are a leader in the church and you have not recognized that the sheep all around you are carrying guns, then you may have missed a session or two on what it means to wake up to the true depth of human nature. You may not be ready to lead in this work.

Our second layer of personal development as leaders is the ability to be able to endure amid the conflict. True maturity tells us that we can work toward attainment even when we are adversely treated in the process of trying to attain. We can work against rifts and separations in the layers.

Another way of seeing this rift and disconnect is that at some point in our life we begin to recognize that we are capable of sustaining more than one emotion at a time. In fact, we are able to sustain more than one emotion at a time about the same person, event, or thought. We can feel hot and cold about the same thing. This ability to move ahead through the confusion and murkiness that presents itself in life is a measure of strength and tenacity in the leader's heart and mind.

We are all capable of getting off the trail and wandering through the bushes and the thicket. During that wandering we very often do things, think things, and say things that are not really what we want to be doing, thinking, or saying. We just do. A lot of that may be directed at individuals around us; at the people who are trying to lead us on the journey. That wounds people. That wounds leaders. It is a part of the mix.

Add to that that there is also suffering or attack heaped on us from outside the church. Are you ready, willing and able to stay on the path—leading the sheep—when the fire gets heavy (from inside and out)? That is what this is all about.

You are going to take hits because you are trying to bring about a sense of development in other people: you are offering direction and formation. Some will be threatened by your activity. Others will not want to be stretched into this growth and so they will start flailing and thrashing.

Take a lesson from our Master. Jesus was crucified by the very people He came to love and tend into new life. The little chicks that He had hoped to gather together ("O Jerusalem, Jerusalem, you who kill the prophets and stone those sent to you, how often I have longed to gather your children together, as a hen gathers her chicks under her wings, but you were not willing!"—Gospel of Saint Luke xiii, 34.) were the ones who again and again killed those sent—including Him: the incarnate Son of God. It will be no different for us.

When we are younger we can whine things like, "It is just not fair". But, somewhere in the growing up, we learn—partly by learning to identify more deeply with Jesus—that most of the things in life are not what we would consider "fair". The mathematical sureties that we somehow superimpose on life do not have any really bearing on what happens and how it happens. Because we struggle to do what is right does not mean that we get a pass on persecution. As we tend to learn—perhaps all too late—it seems instead to invite it. This is why it is the final portion of the heart of the leader. All of these other traits are a part of the heart of being a leader; but know this, the final test your heart must pass is to do all of these things even after people have begun taking pot shots at your for being a leader in the first place. Love them even as they nail you to a tree.

This idea and this tenacity bring us back to the beginning of this section. The first and most central piece to the heart of the leader—the one trait that sums them all up—is love. Love even while being persecuted. Can you love (and do the right thing by loving) even when they are going after you and are at your throat?

I am reminded of Mother Maria of Paris when I think of this kind of love. This woman—an Orthodox nun—sheltered and hid German Jews from the Nazis. She smuggled Jewish children out of the ghettoes in garbage cans. She forged baptismal certificates to aid Jews in getting out of the country. She continued to help even when she was taken to a prison death camp and was tormented there. She continued on with The Resistance right up until the moment she died in the camps. Do you have that kind of tenacity to do what is right? Can you love into your own death?

> *A leader recognizes that they are a target for being persecuted and silenced because of who they are. A leader who loves to do what is right is willing to die for the love they share—even at the hands of those they teach.*

Connectivity Toolbox
—Stuff for your Journal

- Write about (in your journal) times you have tried to care for the "little chicks" in your care and have instead felt as if you have been attacked. What was it that you were being attacked for? In terms of righteousness, were you trying to help people move closer to God on the journey? Were you acting out of self-ambition or pride? How did you respond to the rants and rails of the people who were attacking?

- List (in your journal) people that you have nailed to a tree in your own growth in the faith. People that you have persecuted because they were doing something you did not agree with. What were the things that you criticized them about? Have others found the same things wrong with you?

- Google "persecution of early Christians" and read up on what a couple of the links present as material. Write about what you find in your journal. Reflect on what it must have been like to have been killed for the faith? How does this compare to the way we persecute others ourselves?

- Fill a few pages in your journal with the things you think are at the root of why we persecute other people. What ways could we learn to communicate that would avoid and circumvent the act of persecution? Are we capable as a species of reducing this urge to scapegoat?

- *"The perennial temptation is to scapegoat rather than to carry the dark side of things. Demonizing the other makes us feel superior..."* Richard Rohr, OFM in "Job And The Mystery of Suffering". Copy this quote in your journal.

- Expound on the quote above—in your journal. Take the words that you put down on paper and share them with your group, using everyone's journal entries on this quote as grist for the mill of the discussion.

- Take the list of people you have persecuted or nailed to a tree in the above toolbox exercise and contact a few of them, asking for forgiveness and telling them how you have grown since that time in your life. Share how this went with the group.
- Workbook pages at: http://feedmysheepleadmysheep.blogspot.com/

Part Two

The Mind of the Leader

18

Wisdom

WISDOM IS ABOUT BEING able to pierce into the depths of an issue. It is being able to gather together all of the truth of a thing—in one place—and then apply all of it to an understanding of the nature of that thing. It is a pooling and collecting of truth and a holding onto of that truth within. In many ways it can be understood as the revealing of things that have been hidden or unknown—"secret wisdom".

We use wisdom when we need to make a choice, to judge, or to decide. We consider it to be the action made in light collecting the best knowledge and data on the issue at hand. We also consider it to be the place we have gathered together all the resources around and about an issue our wisdom place. It can also be the "deep air of being" that attends gathered truth and understanding.

Wisdom is breaking a thing down into the smallest possible pieces, revealing how and where everything is interconnected and interacts with everything else. Wisdom is knowing and understanding (or being able to get the knowledge and get the understanding) how all of the pieces fit together.

There is a whole developmental spiritual nuance that is connected to the "idea" of wisdom as the feminine principle in the cosmos. This is Wisdom as the mate or consort of the Divine Father. In the Old Testament and inter-testamental period of time it was equated with the Shekinah glory or the Kabalistic concept of "Hokmah". There is a lot of murkiness around this belief and it is veiled in a thousand forms of confusion because it has deep reaching implications that people have felt uncomfortable with. Because the idea of a feminine principle in God sounds so much like sexuality and also dualism, flags and alarms went up and off all over the theological community (and still do).

Some early Christians spoke about the Holy Spirit as this feminine side to God. Others saw the LOGOS as the embodiment of this wisdom-principle from the Old Testament known as Sophia. Still others spoke of Sophia as a whole separate being in the cosmos that may or may not have had a share of Divine Being and Essence. I hesitate to bring these matters up because there is so much diversity and conflict surrounding them, but I do want you to know that wisdom is something that is very revered in our Judeo-Christian history. It has often had a place in "personhood".

Wisdom is a central and core issue in spirituality and it tends to revolve around the areas in which God connects to and with mankind. Wisdom is somehow a bridge between God and man. I will leave the mystical discussion at that. It is however, a topic worthy of a study all its own for all believers, in all places, and through all time.

For purposes of the work we are doing here, let us drill down a bit into the idea of wisdom surrounding leadership. Where do you go to find out about the call you live under to lead people to Jesus and to feed them? How do you work with growing in this capacity? Where do you go to shop for the food you need to become wise in leading? This is one way of looking at amassing wisdom about or around a thing.

I have to admit, when I think of wisdom I think of Job. I know King Solomon stands out as the deliverer of the most intelligent and pithy aphorisms about wisdom, but the story of Job cinches the whole thing for me. It is a more visceral telling of wisdom. The part that is the apex of the wisdom-tale (in my mind) is when God steps up and deliverers the wisdom-ultimatum to Job. God has been around Job and his alleged buddies for some time—listening to all they had to say or thought they had to say. At this point, speaking directly to Job-the-now-solitaire, the scripture says,

> [1] "Then the LORD spoke to Job out of the storm. He said:
> [2] "Who is this that obscures my plans
> with words without knowledge
> [3] Brace yourself like a man;
> I will question you,
> and you shall answer me.
> [4] "Where were you when I laid the earth's foundation?

> Who stretched a measuring line across it?
> ⁶ On what were its footings set,
> or who laid its cornerstone—
> ⁷ while the morning stars sang together
> and all the angels[a] shouted for joy?
> ⁸ "Who shut up the sea behind doors
> when it burst forth from the womb,
> ⁹ when I made the clouds its garment
> and wrapped it in thick darkness,
> ¹⁰ when I fixed limits for it
> and set its doors and bars in place,
> ¹¹ when I said, 'This far you may come and no farther;
> here is where your proud waves halt'?" (Job xxxviii, 1–11.)

This questioning/grilling of Job by God goes on and on for several chapters. When it is all over—somewhere in the beginning of chapter 42—Job peeps out a somewhat humble and valiant response. He basically says that he was wrong to have assumed that he knew anything and that he will hold in tension (in the future) his knowing with an understanding of how much he really does not know at all.

This is wisdom. Gather everything you know about a thing around you. Believe it with everything you have. And, at the exact same time, hold in contention the fact that you have absolutely no idea about the meaning of things. When you see this balancing act that wisdom requires of us, you get a sense of the pressure and energy that goes into the making of a person who is considered as wise. They know, and they know that they do not know. That is wisdom. And this wisdom is deeply connected to a rich and abiding relationship with the Holy Spirit.

> *Leaders know where to turn to get the wisdom they need to encounter various situations in their lives. They know how to listen to the "deep questions" of life that expose just how much they do not know. They do not find these two things mutually exclusive.*

Connectivity Toolbox
—Stuff for your Journal

- Read Job 38—42. Pause often to reflect on what you hear being said in this set of verses. Read it straight through the first time and then come back to it again, a day later.

- As you read the portion from Job on the second day, grab your journal and write out some of the key concepts or questions you hear being brandished about. Go through the whole of the above selection and record these observations—even if it takes more than one sitting.

- Journal about how the Job passage makes you feel. What is the wisdom that you take away from the reading of these verses?

- In your journal, write about a time when you went through a Job-like loss or period of suffering in your life. How did your friends help? What did they say? Looking back on Job, how would you handle a crisis of loss or suffering in the life of a close friend? What would you say?

- Google "Sophia" on the internet. Write about what you find. Why do you think people had a tendency to personify Wisdom?

- Write a letter of thanks to someone you consider to be wise, someone who has helped you out along the spiritual journey. Make sure to thank them for the wisdom they expressed in your life and let them know how that has helped you.

- Write a poem or draw a drawing (or paint a painting) in your journal that is an expression of wisdom. It could be about a scene from some event or happening that portrays wisdom to you, it could be about the Wisdom or Sophia of God, it could be impressions you have of the trait itself. Whatever first comes to your artist's heart, put it down on paper.

- Workbook pages at: http://feedmysheepleadmysheep.blogspot.com/

19

360° Surveillance

The idea of 360° surveillance is one of my favorite mind traits in leadership. I am no fool; I know it comes from the countless hours I spent playing "army" and "war" at Georgie Acker's house when we were young. One thing led to another and an all day set of "war games/operations" invariably turned into an all night of "manhunt" and "kick-the-can". No matter the form our energy took, getting yourself into a strategic vantage point was what it was all about. You had to be tucked out of sight with a vision of the whole playing field.

It is critical to make sure you have an understanding of the lay of the land in whatever setting you are in. That means an understanding of the physical surroundings from within which you are leading people; but, this also means an understanding of the interior landscape of individuals, the social landscape of the group (dynamics), and the external landscape of either the competition (in business settings) or divergent community groups (the other religious organizations in your area). You have to have a sense of how things are interacting and affecting each other.

If you think of taking a hike and climbing to the top of a mountain you can get a sense of what I am talking about. It is a lot of hard work, sweat, muscle-burn, and focused breathing to get to the top, but what a view when you get there. If you pick the right climb, you can get a panoramic vista that gives you the whole 360° view. And that is worth the climb.

From that kind of vantage point you can see how things fit together. You can see exactly where town lines are, where creeks and rivers flow through the villages, where flooding is likely to happen, how the population is distributed, areas of potential damage from the elements, easy access points, and areas that are sheltered or hidden from other places.

It is amazing. You really get a whole different sense of things when you climb to a vantage point.

One of the things I love checking out from vistas or high climbs is how a river may be—or may have been—changing its shape from a side-winding bed to a series of cutoffs and short-cuts. Rivers—over thousands of years—change back and forth between side-winding and straight-shots. It is a series of processes that come as a result of flooding and build up of sediments over time. All of geology reveals this sense of evolutionary change that you can see when you get to a high enough point.

It is no different in our lives. There are places we can get to in order to watch, study, and observe the lay of the land in front of us. As a leader, do you ever just watch the group? Do you ever spend time watching the individual members in this setting or in other settings? Have you known people over time? How have they changed (like a river changes over time) as a result of the varied processes and "geologic forces and changes" in their own lives?

From the top of the mountain, you can see the bear that is 500 feet down the trail from the youth group that is hiking unaware. You can see the gasoline truck that is stuck on the railroad tracks two miles down from the speeding passenger train that is headed for disaster. You can take stock in all that is going on and see how one thing influences another. A good vantage point not only helps to avert danger, but it is an invaluable tool in making sequential plans that rely on dependencies.

If you are in a group, taking a quick 360° survey of the room will help you to see what examples you will want to use to drive home the points of the discussion or the activities you are about to embark on. A good leader will tailor those examples to the group that is present. You have to be able to sweep the room visually to identify the participants, but you also need to have an interior survey of the groups' lives so the examples you site make sense and drive home the points you are making. So, it is not only good enough to have a working knowledge of what you see, but of what drives and supports the interior mechanisms of what you see. What major life influences are your members facing? Do they share any cultural or social biases or similarities? Do they all speak the same language? These are some simple surveillance questions. You will need to work out more of them for your specific group.

There is one particular view that you must always remember when talking about 360° surveillance. It is the view behind you. Many people get to a vista and see that panoramic view in front of them extending out to the edges of their periphery, but forget to look behind them. This is a key mistake in surveillance (another is not looking up). If you do not look behind you, you may miss an intruder that is sneaking up on you. You get such an elevated and lofty feeling at being able to take in the entire forward landscape; you forget that your back is wide open. Boom, you get struck from behind.

In the metaphor of the group, this means you have got to check into the historic elements of the group and its processing. Where has the group been before? What have they done? Where have they failed and succeeded in the past? What about the individual members? What have they been through and what were their successes and failures? How about you? What has worked or not worked for you with leading groups in the past? What have your experiences been like as an individual group member in the past? All of this is what is going on behind you as the leader. All of this impacts you and the group your are leading.

> *A leader realizes the need to get a vantage point from time to time. From this place above the fray of things they can take stock in how things look, how things fit together, what things are hidden from the view below, and which things you may want to avoid or work around. A leader also makes sure to learn about what is behind him and the group—what is in the past.*

Connectivity Toolbox
—Stuff for your Journal

- Take your journal on a hike up a hill. When you get to the top, list all of the things (in your journal) that you can see from this vantage point that were not available to your view from down below. Be detailed about specific things you had no idea existed from your view below.

- In your group (a group you lead) there are some specific things that your group members do not see about each other or know about each other because they are members of the group and not the leader of the group. List some of these things out about each person (in your journal). Also list about one or two dozen observations about how your group interacts with each other. Things that you notice as a leader that they members may not be aware of.

- Google "vantage point definition". Copy the definition in your journal. Make sure to go to a couple of sites and add pieces of the definitions they offer that are different from the first.

- Write a letter to a friend (in your journal) in which you describe the value of having a vantage point to view your group (the group that discusses this handbook material) from. Write about some of the things you have learned about your group by taking the view from this "vantage point".

- Draw a map of your group in your journal. Lay it out as if it were a topographical map of a set of mountains and valleys. Label where all of the people are in the group. Identify what kind of feature they are and why (Bob is a cliff because he is solid, Harriet is the path because she helps to facilitate people's growth so well).

- Copy (in your journal) the poem found at: http://farsidebanksof jordan.blogspot.com/2009/12/river-bending.html. Discuss impressions this poem leaves with you about our topic.

- Workbook pages at: http://feedmysheepleadmysheep.blogspot.com/

20

Goals and Priorities

THE BACKBONE OF MAKING any advances in life is setting out on the journey with a map. Even if you just show up in the terrain of life with a blank piece of paper and a pencil—beginning the sketches that will transform themselves into a cartographers dream—a map is vital for direction, aim, accomplishment, development, and even simple sightseeing. Showing up with the desire to figure out where you are going is also enough—since the mind will begin to record where you have been and interpret what lies ahead of you. After all, this is what a map is.

Although ambling is beautiful, when you get to the place where you are able to visualize the fullness of the playing field, then direction is possible. When they are acknowledged as vital for the journey, goals and priorities (just like a map) make the journey all the more memorable and lend focus for discovery. They can also help us cram more into life when that is required.

So many people go at life without setting and acknowledging clearcut goals and priorities. Some say that, "they do not want to look at life so formally", so "business-like". What they do not see; what is just below their radar of understanding is that they are making goals and striving toward them whether they acknowledge those goals and priorities or not. Not making goals and priorities—not choosing—is a goal and priority. It is the goal and priority of not being prepared.

When we consciously look at the process of moving through life, we tend to develop a more cohesive understanding of our lives and a better view of the terrain we inhabit. Setting goals and priorities is one step in obtaining that conscious overview and reflection of our lives. Setting goals and priorities is about being prepared and establishing check points in our lives.

A goal is simply a projected hope. It is something you long to get done, see, accomplish, taste, handle, hear, or bring into your life in some way. Making a goal out of a yearning is taking it and fashioning it into a statement. "I want to see Yosemite before I die". "I want to take my family out for breakfast before church". "I want to see my son in his new home." Now these may not be specific renderings of a statement of hope, but they are statements of hope none-the-less.

The better you get at setting goals and accomplishing them, the better honed and focused your statements about your hopes will become. It is a gradual growth thing. Like the rest of leadership. What you may see as a goal at this point in life may shift and become a sub-goal or a priority at another point of life.

I think it helps to add a few more words to our understanding of goals. There was a classic leadership book that came out in the mid-seventies entitled "Strategy for Living". Long before the millennial push to understand and jargonize the art and discipline of leadership, this book set out to help Christians learn to use structural and organizational tools by setting goals and priorities in our everyday lives. It was written by Edward R. Dayton and Ted W. Engstrom. I remember using the book with the leadership team of our community youth group. It changed my life. Some of the key words that these fellows used to organize a personal strategy were: "purpose", "goals", and "priorities".

A purpose is an underlying meaning to life; like: "I want to be a good father". A goal is something that you can do (remember a concrete statement of hope) to help you live that purpose; like: "I want to spend 10 minutes each morning with each of my sons (separately)—having devotions". Priorities may either be little sub-goals under each goal; like: "I want to study the Sermon on the Mount with them, first; the Fruit of the Spirit, second; and, the Golden Rule, third." Or, priorities can also be setting a long list of goals into a ranked order: "My first goal is . . . , second goal is…, third goal is…".

There are countless other goal-systems out there. What is important in any or all of them is the basic structure of the process—no matter what words you use. There should be large and looming statements that represents your hopes and dreams. You should be able to drill down into those hopes and dreams and come up with some concrete goals that are measured steps to accomplishing your hopes and dreams. Then, finally, there should be some way to make a list of prioritized actionable items under each goal.

A lot of people do not go at this process because they fear failure. Anyone who has worked hard at this process knows that failure is a part of the process. It is not something to be feared. It is something to be expected and leveraged in order to move ahead. The only way you will get better at writing or stating goals is to be really bad at it for a while and then to use the edginess that comes from the frustration of not achieving your goals to improve them. Success is a cumulative thing that builds on momentum of failure.

Imagine the possible difference in the lives of individuals if every church would sit down with their congregations and taught them how to set and refine goals. Doing it in age appropriate groupings would stimulate discussion of common hopes and dreams and would give concrete platforms for people to get closer as they shared in and worked on common goals. It could move us further into intimacy with Jesus and the Trinity.

> *A leader knows that people are making goals and priorities in their lives every minute of everyday—whether they acknowledge it or not. The leader knows that to set and establish those goals and priorities as lucid and conscious portions of life will only enhance the journey and possibility of achieving them with a measure of satisfaction and success.*

Connectivity Toolbox
—Stuff for your Journal

- In your journal list three goals you have for the remainder of this study of leadership.
- Under each of the goals that you have listed in your journal (above) list 1–3 priorities that will help you get to these goals.
- Draw a map of your life in your journal. Be sure the map includes where you have been, signposts along the way, where you are headed and milestones you wish to achieve. Be creative with the landscape. Include a key to interpreting the map as well.
- Dayton and Engstrom wrote a sensational book on goals and priorities entitled "Strategy for Living". Google the book and see about picking up a used copy on-line. It is a must for a leadership library.
- Go out and buy a small but durable tablet or mini journal. This will become your *"Must Read Before I Die List"*. Make sure your start it off by listing out 10—20 books that you have got to read before you die. Share your titles with your group that is studying this book.
- List (in your journal) 10 failures you have had in your life.
- Under each of the above failures in your journal, list some hypothetical goals that may have helped you attain and achieve a different outcome.
- Copy this quote by **Edmund Hillary in your journal**: *"You don't have to be a fantastic hero to do certain things—to compete. You can be just an ordinary chap, sufficiently motivated to reach challenging goals."*
- Write about the above quote in your journal. Make sure you Google Edmund Hillary and find out who he was and how this quote exemplifies his life.
- Workbook pages at: http://feedmysheepleadmysheep.blogspot.com/

21

Vision

THERE IS NOTHING THAT drives a soul like vision. All of the hungering and thirsting toward anything in life comes from having a vision planted in us. That vision comes from some experience we have had—the seed is dropped into the soil. It gets watered by everything that comes our way. If we take care to nurture it, it will become the force that keeps us bound to God throughout the trials that await us. Without vision, leaders are limp and lifeless fish floating on the surface of the pond—wherever the wind blows them. Those kind of fish not only look gross, but they stink—real bad. Vision is a deep goal—fastened in the soul with a hope that springs eternal.

The vision that has come into my life has always been related to deep woods experiences. Jesus got a hold of my soul when I was at a summer camp program in the Poconos. I spent several weeks each summer at a faith-based camp and learned to live like a disciple out and in the wilderness of the Pennsylvania portion of the Appalachian Chain. There is a straight line from my heart into the heart of God and it pierces through the beauty and grandeur of nature along the way. My vision of spirituality, formation, and direction always involves the out of doors and always involves retreating from the hugger-mugger to get a sense of perspective.

As we start to think about vision, we are going to recognize that it is connected to our getting to a vantage point. When we find out how we are going to get away and above enough to take notice of the lay of the land; that thing we end up sensing inside—when we look out over the vista—that is our vision. When we get to the place where we can see; what opens up inside of us? What deep thing drives our very soul to God?

When I stand on my inner promontory, what opens up in me is a sense of awe, beauty, wonder, radical amazement, and humility. I am dwarfed by the glory of the LORD of the trees and rivers. The one who etched the Appalachian valleys into the planet stands firm and unmoved in decisive creativity. My vision is wrapped up in pines and trails, woods and rivers. I know that I am at my best when I live from the dirt.

Trying to find out where we are most primal in our connection to Jesus will help reveal to us what our vision is wrapped around. Some people will have their vision wrapped around the city, around social issues or conflict resolution. Some will have a vision connected to family growth, or economic stability for the poor. The vision takes a thousand shapes, but it has a shape and it is a core motivator in our lives. Not to know our vision is to be blind. Once we know our vision, we have a place to begin from at every juncture in our lives.

As a leader, vision is what will magnetize or draw a crowd. We tend to put our vision out there and the people who resonate with a similar calling or seeing of the world will collect around us because they feel at home. It is critical is to acknowledge that this is how people tend to group; and then, remember that it is the shared vision from which we lead not from our egos. When we isolate the common vision as the magnetic pull of groups, then we are making sure to take the leader's ego out of that position.

Many a group does not openly acknowledge the center of their shared vision—their common sight. After floating around in the murky waters of confusion, they eventually just become enthralled with the leader and think that the leader is what is magnetically calling to them. It is in fact something that leaders themselves can fall prey to as well. This illusion comes from lack of clarifying what it is that unites us in our calling.

Each group must go through the hard work of finding their vision. Even Christian groups have slightly altered ways of seeing their calling in Jesus. Some will tend the homeless because of their vision. Some will hold hands with the dying because of their vision. Some will emancipate government because of their vision. But, it is vital to be about the task of talking about the shared and common vision at our centers. It cannot be the leader that holds a group together; it must be the shared vision.

One of the great ironies of life is the modern Evangelical movement. Many of the leaders within the diverse rendering of Evangelicalism rail against the primacy of the Pope in the Catholic Church or the devotion to the Spiritual Father in the Orthodox Church because it seems too cult-like and too much like idolatry to them. They are screaming and raving about how these traditional figures are imagistic of the anti-Christ personality; all the while they are building towers of Babel for their own personality. They climb higher and higher above the crowd, drawing more and more attention to their ego and are screaming about how "them over there" is wrong. Alas and alack, they are sharing a vision with their groups and churches—the vision is of them as god. They are saying one thing and doing another.

Reverend Dr. Martin Luther King, Jr. is one of the leaders that best exemplify this idea of unifying vision. He drew people around a vision not an ego. His speeches clearly painted images of common scenery that lived within the collective hearts and minds of many, many people. He could rally people around a common vision of freedom for all mankind. He put it out there, and reminded people often that his vision was a vision that he shared with them—he shared with us—it was not a seeing of one man's ego.

A leader recognizes that vision is a magnetic pull within individuals. We tend to feel drawn to and comfortable with people who share similar vision with us. A leader helps unify people around this shared vision, not around their ego.

Connectivity Toolbox
—Stuff for your Journal

- Write in your journal about your vision. What is your vision? What is at the core of your hope in life? List ten words to describe your vision. Where did this vision come from? How was it planted in your life? How does it drive you and affect others?

- Google "I have a dream" by Rev. Dr. Martin Luther King, Jr. Print out the full text of the speech and read it. Underline or highlight portions of the text that "ring out" in your heart and mind and soul.

- Copy the portions (into your journal) which you underlined or highlighted in the speech above.

- List ten things in your journal that describe the type of vision that Dr. King is sharing with the people of his day.

- Do any of the things you listed in your journal as descriptors of Dr King's vision relate to you and your vision? How about to the common vision of your book discussion group? How about to groups you lead?

- Write an essay in your journal about what you think makes up the vision of Jesus in the New Testament. If you had to outline His vision so you could share it with His disciples, what would that look like? Write that outline at the end of the essay.

- Copy this quote of John Muir's into your journal: *"When we try to pick out anything by itself, we find it hitched to everything else in the universe."* Write about the "vision" in Muir's quote above (in your journal)

- Workbook pages at: http://feedmysheepleadmysheep.blogspot.com/

22

Encouraging Others

I FIND IT HARD to believe how much certain things impact us. They get inside us and drive us forward; often with little recollection or acknowledgement of their presence by our alleged rational and reasonable consciousness. There was something that one of my youth leaders said to me on my first break during the autumn of my freshman year that seems to have been responsible for me writing this book. She shared a piece of her struggle that changed my life.

We were sitting at the local diner back home—the scene for many deep and altering sessions of direction and formation in those days—with our journals cracked wide open. We were ready to write down any profound words or intelligent forays either one of us made. I remember writing down one of those laconic and lapidary statements that she made. She was sharing openly about her own struggles with leading in the life of the church. This honesty encouraged me to wrestle with what she was saying: like Jacob did with the angel. What I did not know was that her words crept out of my journal and deep down into the recesses of my sub-conscious mind/heart and have been driving me forward for the past thirty-two years. Those words made a deep wound in my soul. This was a healing wound (if you can imagine the opposition of those words together); a mark that scar tissue of glory and power has collected around. It was an odd wounding of my soul. It averted me from a direction of ego building leadership and delivered me to a subconscious process of direction and formation.

She said, "Every Christian leader has one task, one call to tend to. We are to lead people to Jesus and let Him do the work with and in them. We have to get out of the way. We/I have to learn to get out of the way and let Jesus do the work." Not only was she right, she actually led me to Jesus in that simple phrase and got me on the path to a lifelong love-affair with God. One small statement was really all she made. Thirty-two years later, and I am still digesting its import and being nourished by its nutrients. Most of the time it was in there, just below the surface; I was not aware of its impact. That was fruitful encouragement.

This encouragement came out of her being candid about her spiritual struggle. It was an encouragement that arises from telling your tale to another. There is another kind of encouragement that arises in life, as well. It is an encouragement that comes from listening to others tell their tale. Neither case is about solving problems and making lists of solutions. This kind of encouragement has faith that the soul is able to intuit how to get on with life; all we need do is be vulnerable with each other and let the Holy Spirit do the work.

This is different than what most people see as "encouraging others". This form of encouraging others is about opening a path toward trust and freedom. This is not the same as cajoling people into ways to stand up for themselves—which is what most people think of when they think of encouragement.

It is not some "ooooooooing" and "aaawwwwing" and telling people how much they "deserve better than that" in life. It is not bandwagon propaganda that touts our victimization and declares we have rights to more. That short sighted and unrealistic egoism is bantered about today as if it were Gospel truth. This is not encouragement at its center. It is an attempt to help people move ahead and press on, but with no guts or real substance. Encouraging others validates the difficulty of the journey and sets people free to get on with the journey. It bolsters the heart it does not rile it up. There is a difference.

There is a sense, in this kind of chatter that you hear all of the time that people are not really engaged with the other person in the discussion. They are not listening to the other person. They are not responding to the other person. What they are doing is hearing the words and then talking about themselves. The information comes in and then the other person is blocked out and all of the rest is just self chatter about our own fears of being treated like that and how we will not stand for it.

You know what I am talking about. We have all overheard someone (sorry to say) chatting away furiously on their cell phone with someone else. They are ranting and raving about how that person should not stand for "that kind of behavior". They need to "end the relationship immediately". Or "quit". Or, "get out, now". Of course, the whole while they are checking the prices on the baked beans and picking up the coupons they dropped or running over your toes with their cart. This is divided mind talk. There is a lot of it today. People think they need to deliver people from their bondage.

This pseudo-encouragement does not reach out in true love to encourage. It just gets people all whipped up and walks away. Churches are full of this. There is no sense of trust and freedom in pseudo encouragement; just hubris and pride. How many alleged conversations that are supposed to be encouraging others are nothing more than finger pointing episodes; one group assigning blame to another? This is not encouragement. This is persuasion.

Encouraging others begins and ends in their story and in their struggle. It is filled with more silence than anything. It is filled with a deep listening. It is not filled with a frantic racing mind that is trying to find examples of how the same thing happened to you. It is an open acknowledgement of how difficult the person's journey is and then a "giving of courage" to them to feed them in the days ahead. It is not giving out adrenaline; it is giving out courage.

We can give courage by sharing hope. We can give courage by planting seeds of confidence. We tend to like to give advice and tell people what we have done to be set free from the wiles of the thing they are experiencing. I think this is cheap grace. What encourages people the most is being heard. People gain some sense of strength from knowing that others hear their anguish.

Most often true encouragement sounds something like this: "WOW. You really have a lot going on. It has got to be tough." Or, "I can't imagine how difficult that is." These statements meet the angst of the other with a large and open heart; not a list of things to do. It may also sound like you sharing your own angst with another, letting them know about the difficulty you are facing in life now (not shared at the same time they are sharing their angst, but on a separate occasion). These two forms of encouragement are really about living from a place that is vulnerable. We are acknowledging the overall brokenness of being human.

In my example above, my friend shared her open angst about where she was in her journey. It went deep into me in a way I did not understand at that moment. Her vulnerability and brokenness encouraged me to take courage and wrestle with life. It could have also happened if I had been the one who shared my soul with her in open risk and vulnerability. True encouragement comes from being in the presence of brokenness with others—standing together in our own woundedness. It is advanced when we do not avert our eyes from what the other is sharing (or we are sharing) by changing the subject. It becomes courage when we simply exist in the vulnerable space together.

> *A leader knows that vulnerability and brokenness are an important part of offering encouragement to others. When we listen or share from this place people can take courage because there is no haughtiness present to mask the desire to help.*

Connectivity Toolbox
—Stuff for your Journal

- Make a list in your journal of all of the people you can remember that encouraged you in life.

- Make a list in your journal of all of the people you have encouraged in life.

- Go back to the two lists above and put a star next to every example of encouragement where you feel like the person doing the encouraging was out of the way and was truly offering courage to the person they were listening to.

- Write a short piece in your journal about the things you believe happen to a person when they "feel heard" by the people in their lives. What does it do for them?

- Google the "Greek word for encouragement". Write out the definition you find for the Greek word (in your journal).

- How does the definition you wrote out above impact your understanding of what it means to encourage? How can you incorporate that definition into the one described in the chapter above? Discuss this with your group.

- Make a list of five people that are very important to you in your life (in your journal). Next to each individual in the list, write out one thing you can do to let them know that you are aware of some struggle they are involved in or some adversity they are working through.

- Choose at least two people in your list above and send them a note or do something else to let them know you "hear" their struggle. Maybe you could invite them to just get together so you can listen.

- Workbook pages at: http://feedmysheepleadmysheep.blogspot.com/

23

Confrontation

THE CLASSIC LINE FROM Pauline theology that sums up how we are to "be" when it comes to confrontation—or what is most often called "accountability" today—is that we are to speak the truth in love. Wow. Such a simple verse to remember; it is almost bumper-sticker like in tenor. But, it is so very difficult to perform this act of grace by speaking truth in love to someone else. In fact, this is one of those areas that you should just expect at the outset to fail at when you are leading. Almost invariably, young or new leaders long with all their hearts to help others that are in their care, but end up posturing themselves harshly or saying the wrong things. That is how it happens. This is how we learn.

I would like to think, however, that we can provide some refinement to our leadership early on by using a little discernment. Rather than jumping right in with both feet when you see a situation that requires a measure of accountability or confrontation, step back and wait. This is the first step on the path to helping others in regards to identifying areas of conflict that they are participating in. Step back, wait, watch, and hold your tongue.

We must exert a measure of self-control on our own selves before we can enter into a discussion with others about ways in which they may be wandering from the fold. But, chances are this is something we will learn in hindsight. I am not sure it means the same without the failures we first experience when trying to help people with our well-meant errors. Our mistakes drive home the need to change the way we help others in this regard.

I think parenting equips us—if we are attentive to it—with this skill. We learn that there is so much that can be addressed and confronted in relationships within the family: whether it is spouse to spouse, spouse to child, or child to child. So much is going on in a family that there is always bound to be some of it that is conflictual. Stepping back gives you a space from within which to gain clarity of vision, focus, and deliberation over exactly what needs to be addressed.

This stepping back also has another feature. When you do not engage immediately, and you step back (taking to a vantage point), you have the freedom to choose your battles. Every parent knows that you cannot possibly fight a million battles; which is exactly the number of battles that are potentially on the horizon in any group or family setting. You must select which efforts you will infuse with your energies. Pick your battles. This is not easy.

There are times when we need to let people work through the things they are doing—even when we think we can save them some trouble. They need to fail at things on their own. They need a chance to get up off of the floor on their own. They need to feel the angst of hurting others in relationships they have. Without this there can be no impetus for them to improve and strive toward better and more wholesome responses.

On Mount Athos (a holy mountain in Greece with a total of twenty monastic houses) there is an old saying. It comes from the folklore of the place. It is developed from years and years of spiritual fathers on the Holy Mountain meeting with spiritual children and offering them direction and formation. At some point in learning about the Holy Mountain, spiritual seekers tend to ask: "Holy Father' what do you do here on the mountain all day long?" The spiritual father answers, "We fall and get up. We fall and get up. We fall and get up, again."

I am sharing this story for two reasons. First, the definition of our spiritual odyssey could very easily be summarized by the words of the spiritual father in the above example. We fall and get up—over and over again. This means that we all fall and that we may need to allow people to build up the calluses on their knees and palms so that they are better fitted for that falling. We may need to let them get up and try again—by themselves. I am also sharing it because WE are a part of that odyssey of falling. We fall all the time ourselves and we would do well to take up an interior posture that remembers what it looks like from the ground.

When we step back and choose which battles we will fight; and when we remember we are thick with calluses ourselves, we are allowing ourselves to get into a more appropriate posture for speaking the truth in love. We are getting into a humble space from which we can speak not as one who is perfect, but as a sinner who spends a fair amount of time on the ground. We are giving ourselves some distance from arrogance and pride. Both of these enemies are potentially present when we attempt to help someone up from a fall.

Think about it. Pride and arrogance are so easily taken up as means of helping others self-correct. And, we all know that if there is any hint of pride or arrogance in someone who is approaching us to help us self correct, that we recoil and refuse the help. The presence of pride and arrogance is equivalent to saying, "Get up you fool. You have fallen again." This really does not bode well for reconciliation.

In stepping back and choosing, we have the luxury of not only getting a better view of what is going on, but as a leader we are given the chance to pray about the situation and also seek some sound advice (or research) concerning a proper response.

There are of course situations that demand an immediate response. These are situations that reflect a deep sense of hazardousness. These are situations when safety is at risk. If someone is being attacked verbally or physically—bullied—then we need to react immediately. We all know that these situations often bring out "reactions" that surprise us when we see them. We need to always decompress from toxic scenarios and confrontations. This means if you as a leader over-react in the process of trying to provide safety, you need to set things straight with those involved and ask for forgiveness. Remember, we are all a part of the odyssey of falling.

> *A leader knows that stepping back and allowing others to fail is often an essential part of leading. A leader knows that in stepping back they can choose which issues to confront and also can get themselves into a humble posture for speaking the truth in love.*

Connectivity Toolbox
—Stuff for your Journal

- In your journal write about a few times in your life when someone has confronted you about some form of conflict in your life. How did that feel? What did they say? Was it a peaceful event in your life or chaotic?

- In your journal write a simple story about a fictional example of a person who has fallen (actually or metaphorically) and the person who comes to help them up. Share it with your group that is studying this book.

- Write a few paragraphs in your journal on why it is better to speak the truth in love face to face as opposed to via email or letter or over the phone. Share these with your group that is studying this book.

- List out (in your journal) ways of confronting people that are inappropriate.

- List out (in your journal) ways of confronting people that are appropriate.

- The 1960s were filled with a lot of confrontation between groups and individuals. Google "1960 confrontations" and select one confrontation to read about. How did it go? Did people step back and seek an appropriate posture before engaging?

- Copy this quote from Richard M. Nixon in your journal: *"Let us move from the era of confrontation to the era of negotiation."* Write about the above quote in your journal. Spend some time writing about the "warlike" implications of the word "confrontation". How can confrontation be stripped of its militaristic and forceful connotations?

- Workbook pages at: http://feedmysheepleadmysheep.blogspot.com/

24

Consistently Recharging

ONE OF THE GREATEST aspects of the digital age is the deepening of our understanding of the mind and communication based on the structure and processes of computers and the technology related to them. They have given us whole new metaphors on how we store data (in our minds and hearts) by visually identifying for us the way in which we need to mechanically save and file data in computers. Drives and folders, applications and downloads all speak volumes about interior human processes—new light on the old ways we spoke about our minds. Recharging and syncing are powerful images of things we need to do in order to stay up to date in our "computer driven lives".

We would be lost without the daily plugging in of our mobile, hand-held, and other digital technologies. The units we use to store data, communicate, and find information would have no available energy to run their applications if we did not recharge them. They may function without wires, but they still need an energy source. Think about what that says about the human mind, the human heart, the human soul, the human spirit, and the human body; it is the same. We need to plug-in to something to recharge our systems—REGULARLY.

The life of the leader is the life of ongoing and constant processing and serving. We are always figuring out how we may best serve the growth in others and learning new ways to perform the service of hooking people up to Jesus and making sure they are led and fed. We are feeding and leading, feeding and leading, feeding and leading again. It is tiring. We are listening to Jesus and to His sheep most all of the time in our leading and feeding. Think about how much energy it would take to physically lead people around all day and stop on occasion to feed them. It would be endless.

We can acknowledge that a certain amount of our processing and serving does come with its own rewards. The things we do to lead and feed others do give us some nourishment. But, on the whole, serving the LORD by leading and feeding His children takes far more from us than it returns to us. This is not a bad thing. This is not a sign of failure. It is a law of energy and physical existence. The intelligent leader does not deny physics, but acknowledges it and sees to the replenishing of his/her energy levels by plugging into the Source to be fed and led themselves.

Everyone clearly has their own ways of recharging. We know that some people are visual and need visual stimulation to grow. Others may be aural, emotive, cognitive, etc.; this will impact the style and nature of the things they do or do not do in order to recharge. At some level, however, everyone needs to shut off the intake of material in order to be fed; and simply rest or "be still". This is difficult for most. We have got to just sit still and grow moss at some level. We need to find some silence—inside and outside.

There are countless practices in the arena of spiritual direction and formation that can facilitate this sort of space inside and out. We can begin with **lectio divina, centering prayer,** or **meditation**—even some forms of **visualization** can lead us to quiet rest and stillness. What is vital is that we work some aspect of stillness into our lives on a regular—daily—basis.

One of the practices that have been a part of the development of Christianity through the ages has been the practice of the Jesus Prayer. Sitting in stillness and silence and repeating the name of Jesus over and over (or the full prayer: "Jesus, Son of God, have mercy on me a sinner") has helped people to calm themselves, soothe themselves, and restore themselves. It is not magic and we are not trying to get God to hear us (as in Jesus' injunction not to expect more from God because of repetitious prayers); we are trying to train our heart and mind to know that our rest and wholeness is in Jesus. We are rebuilt into the new man by our contact with the Way, and the Truth, and the Life. One way we can ignite the remembrance of this contact is by speaking His name often, in the stillness and rest of the heart.

There are an ancient set of teachings about the inner life of stillness and silence. They are known as the ***Philokalia***. They were collected together in the eighteenth century by a monk from Mount Athos, Greece.

His name was Nikodemos of the Holy Mountain. The title of the collection means "love of the beautiful".

The writings in the Philokalia are all about how to enter into the stillness of God and to participate with God there—to become one with God (in as much as we are able to connect with the Energies of God and not the Essence of God). This unification occurs in what the Neptic Fathers (the fathers of "stillness" and "watchfulness") called the process of Theosis (or becoming divinized by God). The process occurs in three stages: purification, illumination, and unification. We are not going to go into detail here on the polemics of the interior life, but we need to know that there was a time when people spoke about the difficulty of becoming like Jesus—the intensity of becoming Born Again. It was not seen as a once and done event, but a daily dying into God and becoming into Jesus.

A serious leader needs to look beyond dumbing down the process of our salvation and delve into the complexities of God's mingling Presence in our lives. The journey into a more intelligent faith will always come from resting and being still. Silence and watchfulness are necessary in the life of the believer. It not only recharges us, but it allows us to participate in the image and likeness of God in ways we cannot while we are active. If we cannot take the time to be still, we really have to ask ourselves if we really believe that salvation is a gift that we cannot earn. Otherwise, the way we live looks like we are trying to earn something!

Without diving back into the presence of our Creative Father (through the Son and in the Holy Spirit)—our Source—we cannot become anything, let alone the fullness of the creatures He intended. Resting in God is restorative. It is the still waters of the Psalmists story.

A leader recognizes that there is deep value and nurturance in recharging. It not only gives us the strength to go on feeding and leading, it unites us with the Energies of the One who truly does the feeding and leading in the first place. It unites with the Energies of God.

Connectivity Toolbox
—Stuff for your Journal

- Write a list in your journal of the things you do to recharge your personal interior and exterior human system.

- Out of the list above, how many of those things do you do consistently in some sort of recurring fashion? Write next to those items the frequency with which you do them to help you recharge—every day, every week, monthly, yearly, etc.

- Write a few paragraphs about what Jesus did (in your journal) to recharge on a routine basis.

- Read John xv–xvii (to the end of xvii). Write a few examples (in your journal) of how Jesus envisions this sense of connectedness between us and Him; and Him and His Father; and us and His Father....

- Think about how you currently connect to Jesus and His Father. Share those ways with your group that is studying this book. Make sure to write down things that others do in your journal. Reflect—later—on whether some of the ways that others use to connect may be helpful for your practice.

- Sit still for ten minutes (use a timer). When you are done, write about the experience in your journal. Was it hard? What was difficult? What did your mind do? What about your emotions? Share this information with the group studying this book.

- Go back over your journal and read it from the beginning. Make sure to soak up where you have been. Do you notice and immense changes in your life? How about in your understanding of leading and feeding? Share these with your group.

- Google the following terms and read up on these practices in formation and direction within the Christian Tradition: *lectio divina, centering prayer, meditation* and *visualization*. Practice one or two of them and see how they aid rest and regeneration.

- Workbook pages at: http://feedmysheepleadmysheep.blogspot.com/

25

Celebrating Failure and Success

Most people understand it is a good idea to celebrate success. It gives some positive incentive to kick back, take a look at your accomplishment and gloat in the glory of it all. Most people do not get why you should do the same with failures. If the positive energy that is sunk into reviewing and acknowledging our success was redeemed into a process that could work for looking at our failures too, think of how much we could learn.

If we could make discussing our failures in to a constructive exercise with an eye toward correcting and improving things, think how much further along the road we would be a year from now. If we could stand on top of our failures instead of silently feeling guilt and shame over them, it would be immense. To fall into guilt and shame and self-loathing does not only keep us from being able to correct our failings more quickly, it also impedes the speed at which we can get on with life and produce success again as well.

Guilt and shame and self-loathing are a part of our "re-entrance posturing" as mammals. Exposing our neck like this lets the group know we recognize what we have done wrong. They are an attempt to "rightly humble ourselves" before others. Although it is clearly a mammalian act meant to get us back into the group after we have done something "stupid", it has all the possibility of slipping into a lifelong pattern that enables clinical depression and stilted growth rather than group correction. These posturing emotions are a step toward growth, not lifelong positions. They are a way of communicating how unabashedly ashamed we are of our behavior and that we know we have affected the whole "clan" by our wrong. Living in this state constantly belongs in a therapist's office or on National Geographic. It is not meant to be a place we live in, simple a place we visit.

Living in the shame, guilt, and self-loathing of our failures drags people down and keeps them from getting on with life.

I remember picking up a recent issue of a business magazine and noticing that the whole issue was on failure. Wow! What a great idea. I know there is a lot of controversy over this in the business world; many people there (as in the church and therapeutic community) argue that it is counterproductive to spend time acknowledging, decompressing, and celebrating our failures. I disagree. I think we will never gain self-mastery or that inner vantage point if we are not able to dissect our lives and see how it is and why it is we get from "a" to "b" in our lives. If we do not know why we are failing, we will probably never get a handle on the ability to cease failing. "Those who fail to remember the past are condemned to repeat it" (George Santayana).

I think the culprit behind our inability to look at failure is "fear". We are afraid. We feel that talking about things will somehow make them happen again. We believe talking about death brings death; that talking about cancer brings cancer; talking about ways we have failed will make us fail again. Does that sound like intelligent belief? Does that sound like good theology? Charles F. Kettering used to say that even though an inventor failed most of the time, he saw those failures as practice shots for the one time that things worked out. Failures were rehearsals for getting it right. Now there is a healthy attitude.

We should really rethink the value of failure in our lives. There is a thing we do in business practice that is called an after action review. It is basically sitting down after an event, process, or production and taking a look at feedback and results. It is asking, "How did things go?" It is reviewing what could be done a bit differently to improve on the overall picture. It is something that should be done for things that go well and things that go poorly. It is a simple and formal process that can reveal countless blessings and self-revelations.

We should decompress like this after success and after failures. There is nothing to fear. The work we do can only produce more information for helping us to move ahead and find out where we tend to get derailed. Asking the questions can only put us in touch with a deeper side of the things we do. We would do well to do this in our lives as individuals and as groups. Sure, you may need to put a time limit on it so it does not go beyond being helpful. But, it is worth doing.

The ongoing damage we do to ourselves and others that could be avoided by looking at and learning from our failures is staggering. We prefer to glide on by hoping that others never notice that we have failed or that we have not spoken about it. In the end, failure to discuss failure tends to diminish the luster of our successes as well. It also tends to keep us trapped on just this side of making any real progress beyond those failures.

There was a story I read about a company who kept an entire line of products that were recalled because of a failure. They lined the walls along the hallway to the general staff cafeteria with the endless sea of boxes containing the returned items. It was part of a campaign they were running to improve quality control and the hardwiring of "live" information on failure and service dings into their processes. They wanted to discuss how to bring quality control into the mix earlier and more frequently into their processes so they could avoid having this wall of product failures which reflected blips on the radars of their customers. I say this was BOLD.

That is how we must work with failures. Work boldly with them. Learn from them; make proper reparation, and correction when necessary. Ask forgiveness if we have harmed another in the process. Failure is nothing more than a practice shot. If we could take on this posture, if we could teach this perspective, think of all of the bonding and improvement that could be made in the time we now use for shame and guilt and self-loathing. It would be immense.

How we measure our connection to failure as well as success is how those around us will learn to measure their connection. When we model how to learn and celebrate our short-comings, then we are teaching others that it can be done and that they do not need to fear. That is the Paschal Mystery. Anything other than this seems to feel a bit cheap to me.

People that are not able to work through errors and failures tend to be the same people that shut-down early in life and seem to die before they die (and not in a good way). They withdraw from life and get lost in the shuffle. They are hidden and obscured from most of life. Fear takes away any gusto they may have had.

A leader recognizes the value of learning from and celebrating their failures and successes alike. Without knowing where we get derailed—the how and the why of things falling apart—we can never expect to move past that point in our lives.

Connectivity Toolbox
—Stuff for your Journal

- Write about (in your journal) how your family used to deal with failures you experienced as individuals and a group. What did your parents do or say? How about your siblings?
- In your journal, list ten failures that you remember in life. These may be yours or others close to you. How did others respond to the failures? What was your response to the failures?
- Google the definition of "failure". Write down the definition in your journal.
- Write a couple of paragraphs explaining the definition of failure (that you listed above) to a young person. Make sure you identify what it is, but then when you are finished, spend some time sharing how you can deal with failure in order to make an impact for future successes and growth.
- Spend some time writing about or drawing/painting about what failure feels like to you. What is it in failure that you fear? Where do shame and guilt and self-loathing fit into the mix of emotion?
- Once we have felt guilt and identified what we feel guilty about and have confessed that to the proper parties and set out to repair that wrong what use does guilt have for us in moving forward? Does it have any? Discuss this with your group that is studying this book.
- Google "quotes on shame" and copy some of them into your journal.
- Share with at least one person—sometime this week—how a simple failure you experienced has helped you learn about yourself and move ahead toward personal growth and development. Share how it went with your group.
- Workbook pages at: http://feedmysheepleadmysheep.blogspot.com/

26

Honesty and Believability

ONCE HONESTY AND BELIEVABILITY has been broken, you lose your ability to lead with the same momentum you had before the breech in trust. This seems a negative place to begin, but I cannot emphasize enough how the breaking of trust erodes our connection to people, particularly if the leadership relationship is built on a sense of leader as "superior."

At some point, every leader will erode this trust. Every leader will fail. If we set our selves up as superiors, it will be a monumental fail. It makes more sense to me to begin building the leadership relationship on "vulnerability" right at the outset. If people can trust us to be vulnerable, then they will also allow us to fail.

This whole erroneous structure built on the premise of the leader as somehow better than the "follower" is really "old school" and an inadequate form of leading. It presupposes some sort of hierarchy in which the leader is loftier and more complete than the "follower." This is really a deviation from what the biblical images portray leaders to be. Look at the prophets. They were somewhat hideously human characters who pointed the way to God. Not for nothing, but most of them really did not have a pack of friends hooking up with them all along the way because they were true to their calling of moving people toward God regardless of what that meant.

I am not suggesting that leaders need to be anti-social and gruff. What I am challenging is this modern part of the tale we are telling that says, "Leaders have a large following and they are looked on with admiration and favor by that following." It may be that our leading has these components, but it may not. It may start out like this, but it may also start out as "a voice crying in the wilderness." There is just as much leadership in John the Forerunner as there is in Jesus, but it takes a different shape. If you doubt what I am saying, just remember that people abandoned Jesus at the end. So, having a large following is never a sign of accuracy in leading.

If nothing else, we have learned from the recent upheavals in honesty and believability of corporate, religious, and political leaders that every leader is still a human and is capable and likely to produce both good and bad in their lives. What sets a genuine leader apart in my view is the ability to be forthright about our earthiness and fallibility right at the beginning so people are not building a cult-like hierarchy out of our role, but rather a sensible relationship of give and take.

What this whole discussion is getting at is that a leader needs to be honest and believable at the outset. Be honest and believable in the middle. And, be honest and believable at the end of your leading. When people find out something about you that they do not like—and believe me they will (remember even the Son of God had this happen to Him)—then you will have built a framework of vulnerability in the past from which to operate from. You will be consistent with yourself. That integrity is at the base of honesty and believability.

What does this vulnerability look like? It is being open about the fact that we are not perfect. It is telling people what makes you angry when we are talking about anger. It is telling people what makes us sad when we are talking about sadness. It is being honest about the fact that we yell at our kids when we are talking about family life. It is not being overt or morose about these things in order to manipulate people into "following us" it is about acknowledging the fact that we are nothing special. Leaders are people who have the ability to help move people along the journey. Leaders are broken people first—just like everyone else.

Vulnerability is beginning from that place; beginning from a deep knowledge of our woundedness and brokenness before God. Speaking about ourselves in these terms at the outset does not build a tower of seclusion or illusion within which we can hide out. This sort of openness builds honesty and believability. It strengthens the feeling in the center of people that lets them know if what is going on around you is real and accurate. A leader that is always about "not admitting their sinfulness and humanity" is genuinely about building a false image. And, although it appears that people enjoy building, developing, and maintaining these false images in and about their leaders (so they can live them in their own lives); a leader knows that what people really need to resonate with is their own brokenness as reflected in the vulnerability of the leaders in their lives. This is the Paschal Mystery.

This type of honesty and believability is really based on Jesus. Even though He could have gone about preaching His worthiness to be followed (since He is God) He did not. He emptied Himself and became a servant. He became broken for us. He became vulnerable. A Jesus-leader needs to carry that same brokenness into the way they lead. We are called to be honest and believable because it keeps people from "idolizing" us and having false-gods in their lives. We are broken sign-posts and we need to keep peoples' images of us true to that fact. Anything else is self-delusion.

When it comes time for the leader to repent and ask forgiveness for something we have done wrong, it will still upset peoples' sensibilities a bit. But, it will be a momentary ripple in the relationship. It will be based on the fact that most other leaders in the world do not live from this place—making it a part of a learning curve in the lives of the members of the group being led. It will be a "startled at the newness" and awkwardness of this newness. It will not be a ripple based on false hope we have given people that we are perfect. This kind of ripple will pass. In the end, this vulnerability models a behavior of honesty and believability for people that is in keeping with the way God values. It is the basis for any and all repentance in our lives.

> *A leader realizes that being honest and believable requires vulnerability. Leaders do not build up false images of themselves for people to see—they are transparent about their brokenness and woundedness as people.*

Connectivity Toolbox
—Stuff for your Journal

- Copy this quote by Jean Vanier (from "Humble Love") into your journal: *"My heart is transformed by the smile of trust given by some people who are terribly fragile and weak. They call forth new energies from me. They seem to break down barriers and bring me a new freedom. It is the same with the smile of a child: even the hardest heart can't resist. Contact with people who are weak and who are crying out...is one of the most important nourishments in our lives. When we let ourselves be really touched by the gift of their presence, they leave something precious in our hearts. As long as we remain at the level of "doing" things for people, we tend to stay behind our barriers of superiority. We ought to welcome the gift of the poor with open hands. Jesus says, "What you do for the least of my brothers, you do for me"."*

- Write about the meaning of the above quote—in your journal—and discuss this with your group.

- Spend time chatting with your group about the kind of risk involved with this sort of vulnerability—not only for leaders, but for all people in general. How is this a part of the Paschal Mystery of Jesus? Write down key features of the discussion in your journal.

- Read the book: "Becoming Human" by Jean Vanier. Keep notes on the book in your journal.

- Gather together with the group that is discussing this book and review your notes on Jean Vanier's book "Becoming Human". What does the book say about vulnerability? What does the book say about leadership?

- Make a list—in your journal—of things you admire about a vulnerable person. What things set them apart from others? Do the same thing for people who are not vulnerable with others. How do they hide behind a false image—or less than honest image—of themselves? Which do you prefer? Discuss this with your group.

- Workbook pages at: http://feedmysheepleadmysheep.blogspot.com/

27

Communication

COMMUNICATION IS THE MOVING of bundles of energy from one place to the next; the receiving of those bundles by the intended recipient, and then some sort of response. Sometimes this energy is information, sometimes it is feeling; sometimes this energy is words and sometimes it is food. When one thing moves from one place to another, is received, and some sort of assimilation/response happens, then what you have just witnessed is communication.

That is a really broad personal definition of communication, but it is intended to be broad. A lot of things that go on in life are really forms of communication, but are not traditionally thought of as such. We send energy (messages) to our minds, hearts, bellies, souls, friends, enemies, groups, families, nations, etc. all of the time. We are communicating constantly. We are even sending messages into our hard-drives and stick drives and "sd" cards.

All of that sending of bits of energy (in its various forms) is a type of communication. Looking at the broadest base of meaning can really help us gain insight on constant need for communication. This feeding of energy to every possible aggregate of life reminds us that communication is a vital nutrient and a form of nourishment in all of life. There is no survival or sustenance without communication.

Keep in mind that communication of any kind and at any level is a cycle or a process. There is a sender, a recipient, a message, and then an acknowledgement of that message. This circular pattern of sending a message, receiving it, interpreting it and responding back is critical in an adequate understanding of communication. If eating is a form of communication of the mouth to the stomach, then digestion is the assimilation/response of the stomach to the rest of the body. In other words some sort of a response is necessary in a system where the giving and receiving of energy is central.

When we are talking about traditional interpretations of what communication is, that means we expect a sender to send a message and a receiver to receive the message, interpret it, respond back to the sender with a reply or acknowledgement and perhaps send the message on to countless other contacts. It is a cycle that is not complete without a reply or acknowledgement. A dangerous trend in communication that is prevalent today because of email is the absence of the reply or acknowledgement portion of the communication. Many people fail to acknowledge the receipt of the message.

There are many reasons for this. Most often people simply feel it unnecessary. There are some; however, who have learned to use the current ambiguity in consumer tracking. By not acknowledging the receipt of emails, they may be less responsible later on and able to claim ignorance and non-accountability. They simply say, "I did not receive that message"; thereby relinquishing them of any culpability or responsibility in the matter at hand. Although I do believe that some people genuinely overlook, misplace, or forget to open emails, I also know that others are intentional about the smoke screen.

Always make sure that any communication you send—whether with your mouth or your computer—is received and understood. If you do not hear back from someone, you really need to contact them and make sure they received and understood the message. I know it is the receiver's job, but if they fail at this task, you model the behavior by picking up and completing the cycle. You may do well to include a simple statement like, "I had not received any confirmation that you received my message, so I wanted to touch base to be sure." Or, include a line at the bottom of communications that simply states, "Please respond to this message that you have received it and understand." We need to check in with people when we are communicating face to face as well. Asking people if they understand or have any questions is one way to get that feedback.

There is already enough ambiguity in any communication because of the varied usage and meaning of words and the skill level used by individuals to describe accurately what it is they are trying to communicate. We do not need to add any ambiguity to the process by which we send out and return these bundles of energy. We need to streamline and standardize our sending, receiving, and responding mechanisms.

This sort of pronounced adherence to a rhythm to communication feels a bit awkward and forced at the outset, but when a group gets into the routine application of the cycle, then things will never be the same. It opens up clarity and capability in teams and families, groups and meetings. It generally improves the quality of what we are trying to communicate.

Keep in mind that in addition to basic communications about a topic or feeling there are ancillary communications that go on. Let us say that you are leading a study for new believers. There is the whole chunk of information that you are communicating to them at the meeting—perhaps you are talking about prayer. During your time together you periodically stop to check in and make sure people understand what is being said. You ask for feedback. They give it to you, you respond, and on it goes. When they get finished the session; however, more communication ensues. People talk about how you delivered your message, about how impractical it was, how helpful it was, and how "so-and-so" was not there and was probably at another church. More communication goes on about the things you are communicating than simply the things you see and know about. People talk when you are not around.

You get the idea. The first communication cycle is just the beginning. There are countless spin-offs and mutations that will occur; each of them impacting a piece of the faithfulness of the original message. Communication will always be a major issue in relationships/groups because it is a complex and multifaceted expression of who we are as people and as a part of a larger and whole creation. It will always be an item we will need to work on. I laugh when businesses say things like, "We communicate well". It is funny to me because that usually means they do not. The group that is working on their communication skills and processes all of the time is the group that does it well. The group that says, "We are always working on improving our communications" is the group that "gets it".

Keep in mind that words are not all there is. We have letters, newsletter, emails, memos, but we also have body language, eye contact, tone of voice, emotion, silence and so much more that is a part of the energy bundle of communication. It is all communicating.

Making sure to use content and form in a unified way is a major strain on a leader's time and skill. You cannot send news of a tragic death over the phone to an answering machine; it requires face to face contact. You do not need to read the information on a power-point slide to the congregation; you need to condense the point you are verbalizing by making a one line summary and putting that on the slide. Selecting how you say what you say is critical. So, not only is the information you deliver vital, but the way you deliver it is vital as well. Communication is a HUGE endeavor that requires serious and ample consideration by leaders everywhere.

> *A leader recognizes that communication is at the core of everything that goes on in a group. Because of this, groups will always need to improve how they send, receive, and respond to any form of communication.*

Connectivity Toolbox
—Stuff for your Journal

- Google "communication management" and "strategic communication". Take a look at the definitions you find there and write them down in your journal. Go back when you have finished and re-read the definitions, making a bulleted list of the things that communication is all about. Share these with your group.

- Think of one person in your life who communicates well. What is it that strikes you about how they communicate that is making you notice them? Share that with your group.

- Copy this quote by George Bernard Shaw in your journal: *"The single biggest problem in communication is the illusion that it has taken place."*

- Reflect on the above quote for a bit and write a few paragraphs in your journal explaining what it means. Give several example of each of the points you make.

- Share your above comments on the quote with your group.

- Think about how you communicate with people in your life. This week, make the attempt to complete the communication cycle by replying to emails you receive from friends. Let them know you received their note and make some sort of response to it. If someone you contact does not complete the cycle, follow up with them and ask them if they received your message and if so, what they thought.

- Google "communication diagram images" and then click on the Images tab in the far left so you are opening the full page of images. Browse through the page and take a look at ten or twenty different diagrams of communication. Write some observations about the complexity of communication in your journal after viewing the diagrams.

- Workbook pages at: http://feedmysheepleadmysheep.blogspot.com/

28

Focus

The ability to cut out all extraneous activity and hone in on the one thing that demands your immediate attention is not different from multi-tasking. It is multitasking with an eye toward discernment. It is being able to fade in and out of one thing and into another with ease and decisiveness. It is being able to rank order the million and one things that are on your list of concerns (or in your portfolio of projects) and select the one thing you need to do right now and give that thing the attention it needs.

The ability of focus requires that you know when things are ripe and ready to be picked for the fullness of what they can offer. Like knowing when to cash in a stock, focus is about directing your attention to the right thing at the right moment, and being able to sustain that attention on that thing until the work is done. Like other traits, it often gets played off for only one of the elements or layers of what gives it meaning. It is not simply about the ability to fine tune your vision. It is much fuller than that. It is about bringing some fine-tuning to what you are looking at, while still realizing that that one thing is a piece of a larger whole; that there is a lot more going on simultaneously.

Part of this kind of focus is being able to select out one thing out from among others. That requires an underlying ability to ignore things or at least put them on hold. How is your ability to ignore other areas of life that are clamoring for just as much of your attention as the thing you are working on? Developing an open ability to communicate with others the need you have to be focused on this one thing now will be part of how you can clear the decks and devote the proper amounts of time. It helps to be able to let people know when you will get to them and their work. If you can tell people when you will get to them, they are more inclined to let you direct your attention where it is needed at the moment. Being able to rank order the things that are in front of you to do is essential. If you can do that with people, it is more than likely that you will be able to do it with tasks, too. You will be able to put one thing on hold and divert attention momentarily to something else.

The further and further you get into the development of your ability to lead people you are going to see how the traits of the heart and mind are really deeply connected and inextricably bound to one another. This ability to focus is bound to the ability to prioritize and to communicate and those skills are in need of the heart's ability to sense and feel. Sometimes we cannot know when something is ripe for the picking. We must intuit that; we must feel for the right time. That comes from the heart. So, you can see how these pathways in leadership wind and wind and overlap all around the inner and outer terrain. It is a complex thing.

When we look at the word "focus" we tend to connect to the "visual" connotations that come immediately mind, because of how we know the word to be about our physical sight. Because of that, it makes sense to see how it lines up with "vision" and "360° surveillance". Focus is about blending these two and other traits that are about visual clarity and selection. It helps to think about our traits (at this point—since we have amassed a large amount of information about so many) in a broader view so we can refine the specific nuances within each of them. Focus is critical, but it is connected to other skills to gain its fullest meaning.

It is often difficult to get buy-in on how you spend your time as a leader. Other people are vying for your attention and so are countless other things. Those other people are focused on what they are calling into view for their lives: what they need from you. They are not thinking about what is best for you or for the group as a whole. So, lining up your focus with other peoples' focus and the focus of the group requires some good salesmanship and also the ability to wait patiently for everyone to get on board. How will you get others to see the need to shift focus right now; as an individual or as a group? Or, how does a group make a decision as a whole to shift its focus? How will you tell people they are next on your list?

Underlying the ability to focus on something or shift the focus from one thing to another is also the ability to wait and deal with loss. In many cases, the thing that snags people up and keeps them from being able to focus is that they do not have the ability to wait or they do not have the ability to grieve a loss.

The art of focusing on one thing will often produce the passing away of other options. While we are dealing with one thing, other things may slip by. Being able to stay focused on the most important thing may mean waiting while watching something as it disappears from view and from our opportunity. A lot of people break their focus when this happens and try to do "that other thing" that is passing from view. They end up losing that new opportunity and also the one they just stopped focusing on.

That being said, another piece of focus is familiarity with failure. At the outset we may jump from one fading opportunity to another because we do not have the staying power. Because we do that, the things we jump away from may be lost forever and we will have failed in completing them. This building up of a callous around failure and staying power will be the thing that helps us learn focus in the future. It will be there to help us make more accurate assessments about the ripeness of a thing and the timing behind the picking.

There are dangers in losing focus or diverting our attention. These dangers are of injury. We have to be able to weigh these dangers out and include the findings in the information we use to make selections toward what we will focus on. When choosing what to focus on, how do you use "potential danger" or "possible loss" in the selection process?

You should, if you are not already, be starting to get the sense that leadership is a moving and fluid thing. It is an adaptive art based on opportunity and need.

> *A leader realizes that where they are focused is critical. Their attention can only be placed in one focused direction at a time; while still sustaining knowledge of other areas. Choosing where to focus will depend on the combining of several leadership skills at once.*

Connectivity Toolbox
—Stuff for your Journal

- When you focus on something, what happens to the rest of what you are doing? Write about how you responded to the above question—in your journal.

- Discuss the above answer with your group. Be sure to journal about ideas that others identify that are important to you.

- Spend some time with Jesus talking about focus. Ask Him about how He decided what to focus on. Journal about what you hear Him saying to you.

- Journal about the 10 things in your life right now that have your focus. What are they? What areas of your life—in the course of one day—get attention from you?

- What do you think the church you are a part of is focused on? List out 10 of the top "focus items" in the church in your journal. Make sure you are writing the "real things the church is focused on", not the things that you know they "should be focused on".

- Google "yoga eye exercises" and take a look at a few of the sites that offer an example of a couple of eye exercises. In particular the focusing exercises that ask you to focus on near and far objects. Also the exercises that ask you to rotate your eyes from left to right. Write about how these exercises and the activities they suggest may have implications for "vision" and "focus" as metaphoric traits of leadership. Share these insights with the group.

- Write about a time—in your journal—when you lost focus or failed to focus and how that opened you up to potential injury. Did you get injured? What were your options? How did you choose? What other traits and skills did it require for you to aright yourself and get back on target—back on focus? Share these things with your group.

- Workbook pages at: http://feedmysheepleadmysheep.blogspot.com/

29

Innovation

The business world is all a-buzz with "innovation". It is the backbone of a growing market in ideas and commodities; particularly because we love to find the "latest fad" or the "hottest thing"; and we love to make our lives easier and more integrated. Innovation helps us evolve beyond where we are now using the pathways of novelty and development. It helps us set goals, reach out, and yearn toward a "new becoming" for ourselves and all we do.

The entire digital industry is not only built on, but driven by innovation. Anyone who has been paying attention the last twenty years should have a stiff neck from making as many sudden whipping turns with their head as we have had to in order to catch the cavalcade of new products, ideas, and technologies. Times they are a changing. Innovations happen with each breath it seems.

When a market and an economy drive the sense of innovation, then there can never be enough, as we tend to run our markets and economies on greed and rampant warehousing. But, innovation in the development of a soul or of a group must be approached with a solid measure of deliberation and wisdom. Something deep in us must be responsible for the amount of innovation that we allow. Innovation must be tempered with the discerning principles of love and of wisdom. We must carefully select where to innovate.

First, however, we need to produce a healthy and open culture that allows for and encourages newness. Think about the groups you belong to and those you lead. How do you handle new ideas? The Church through time has been a mass destroyer of new ideas. The modern Evangelical Church—which believes it has cut its ties with the "Traditional Church" of the past—has really out done itself with witch-hunts, stake-burnings, and book-burnings as far as I can see. They have surpassed some of the very ideologies they have condemned in the Church that grew out of the Classical Period and the Roman and Byzantine Empires. This fear of change is something that must be addressed if true freedom and growth are to be espoused and endorsed.

The tendency of groups when innovation threatens their sense of identity and stability (either rightly or wrongly) is to cut off any affiliation with the new ideas and changes. They either consider the ideas or holders of the ideas as "dead" to them; or they ostracize or caste them out of the group. These new ideas and their innovators are heresies and heretics. Just read Knox's book **Enthusiasm** to get an historic view of this.

Should we cut off everyone who has a different view? Should we draw lines of heresy and orthodoxy around and through things that are believed by others? Is this vital for survival? Can differences be seen as differences without being good or bad?

At some level, we may need to choose to disagree or choose to "not innovate at this time" because of and for the health of the group or person involved. It may be better for them not to make the changes at this time. I can understand that. What I think has become more apparent over time, and what I would challenge people to reflect on is, perhaps we can send people off with a "freedom" and a "blessing" to do this new thing. Perhaps we can find a way to allow for deviation and not necessarily be so "black" and "white" about options and responses. After all, we do have the advantage of history to fall back on. Sometimes different things are not "evil".

There is a need for weighing and projecting when it comes to analyzing innovative options. We will talk a little bit about risk management in a few chapters; but, you need to recognize some of the risks that you may be incurring by either choosing to innovate or choosing not to innovate at this time. And, this then, becomes the balance you strive for: you provide an openness that encourages innovation and you continuously measure for risk and the tolerance/benefits of this innovation and its growth in new directions.

A culture and environment that straddles this razor's edge needs to be deeply rooted in education. The growing group and leader must be constantly educating themselves. If you are not always about education then there is a good chance that you will miss opportunities for innovation that will drive and feed growth.

A lot of people hear all of the things that need to happen to grow and develop as a person or as a leader and they either shut down or get overwhelmed. It is a lot of work. For the leader who is a Jesus-Leader and a Jesus-Lover and a Jesus-Follower, the hope for balance comes from being open to the Spirit—connected to the fullness of the Godhead.

Our connection to the Trinity is the driving force in our lives. If we are not always growing, then there is a blockage somewhere in our lives as an organism of God—an organism of the Trinity. That blockage needs to be removed. Living things are always growing. If a living thing does not want to grow or does not continue to grow there is something wrong. So innovation in the spiritual life of someone connected to God—connected to the Trinity—is a sign of health; a sign of life.

Think about areas you choose not to innovate in; these may be sensitive areas that you have some deep seated and long standing issues with. You may want to free up some of the soil around these issues so that new life can come out of this soil. The center of the Paschal Mystery is new life springing from old life: life coming from death. Christ has died. Christ is Risen. Christ will come again. That is innovation.

Fear is the reason we do not innovate. What is the fear that is keeping you from growth? What does it reveal to you about your life in the Trinity?

A leader does not fear innovation. A leader provides a freedom and a culture that supports innovation. A leader also speaks to the risks innovation may bring with it and knows when to hold off on changes until a system is healthy enough to sustain the growth.

Connectivity Toolbox
—Stuff for your Journal

- Make a list in your journal of areas you do not have "new life" or "innovation" in your life. Make sure you identify the fears associated with staying away from growth in this area.

- Write about why people fear innovation (in your journal). Be sure to address the two central issues of a culture of freedom and also an ongoing need for education in your discussion. Share these entries with each other in your group meeting.

- List ten (in your journal) of the most innovative ideas you can think of that have come out in *the market* in the past ten or twenty years. What made them so innovative? How did it pay off?

- List ten (in your journal) of the most innovative ideas you can think of that have come out in *the Church* in the past ten or twenty years. What made them so innovative? How did it pay off?

- Talk to Jesus about areas in your life that feel dead. Ask Him how He wants you to respond—how does He want you to innovate toward new life? Write that out in your journal. Get busy heading in that direction. Will it require any changes in your personal culture and freedom? How about in education? What will you need to learn?

- List out- in your journal—the areas in your group (the one/ones you lead—not this discussion group) where you feel blockages to growth. Ask Jesus about changes for these areas and journal about what you hear Him say. Discuss this with the group you are studying this handbook with. See if they have suggestions.

- Workbook pages at: http://feedmysheepleadmysheep.blogspot.com/

30

Circumambulation

CIRCUMAMBULATION IS JUST GETTING out and walking around. In this sense it is mingling with and among folks. It is the practice of getting out, in, and among the people. The practice of getting out, in, and among "your people" is a valuable tool for groups, businesses, and organizations. You get out and among the people and you check on how they are doing, what they are up to, and what they need. You see people while they are busy and you check in with them, making sure they are doing ok.

It is a tool for gauging where things are at with the people you are caring for or serving. It is a way of taking the pulse of the group. It is also a way of directly interacting with people that you may not otherwise run across in your piece of the work you are all doing together; a way of personally touching base, contacting, seeing and listening to people. It is milling about with a purpose.

I think the systemic structure of most organizations—regardless of their focus and purpose—eventually supports the practice of isolation by function. Small groups of people within larger groups of people tend to gather or congregate based on interests or roles and functions and set themselves apart from the rest. Eventually these groupings of people collect other groups of people around them and develop sub-cultures and sub-structures that support their reason for being. This is the way groups grow.

If the leaders of groups do not set the tone and get out and mingle among "the whole" of the group, then the members of the group are less likely to do the same. People tend to settle into what is familiar and comfortable. This habit of "walking around" is one of those practices that will not naturally present itself. It takes time and a disciplined commitment.

But, once established and scheduled into your routine it is something that everyone can become familiar and comfortable with.

It does not matter who or where you lead: a business, and organization, a church, or a family, the idea and activity of getting out into the thick of things and listening to what is going on is possible. It is not only possible, but necessary. The places we go to connect with people are "listening posts". They are pipelines of information that you will incorporate into the future of your leading. These key ideas and concepts that you pick up from people will be the driving force in understanding how the group is doing and in what direction they may need to head. When you get out and walk around, you are entering into the greatest research laboratory at your group's disposal. But, it is not just a pipeline of information, but of relationships as well.

If the groups you are a part of or are leading are particularly large, then you may be meeting with small groupings of people as you wander around. If they are relatively small groups, then you may be mingling among individuals. It does not matter which of these is the case. What is important is that you are meeting with the majority of the people in the group in informal conversations to find out how things are going for them. Keep in mind that it may take a while for people to feel open enough to provide information beyond simple small talk. This is normal. People are trying to gauge whether you are really committed to this idea of listening. They want to make sure this is not just a new fad you are trying.

What this tells us, as leaders, is that we need to be intentional about it and consistent. We need to put it on a calendar or schedule and then be sure to do it when the time comes up. If we start to bump this activity off of the calendar one time because something else comes up (which it always will) then people will not believe that we are taking this mingling seriously and they will not invest in the process. If we take it seriously, the rest of the group will take it seriously as well. This is just another example of modeling the behavior you expect back.

Although the first few times that you "make your wandering" out and among the throngs may be sort of casual and laid back, you will want to bring them around to a focused listening as time goes on. It is a good idea to have a dozen or so stock questions to ask. The questions should be open ended enough that people could answer them in one of many ways. This allows for people to answer the question in whatever frame of mind they are in. If you ask an open-ended question, you can be sure that the answer will reflect immediate and present situations in the life of the person asked. A lot of times people will ask, "How do you mean"? This means you have asked an open-ended question and they understand it is open-ended and they are checking in which direction you want them to go. I usually tell them to answer it "however best feels natural to them". Or, sometimes I say, "That is up to you".

One of the best ways to develop a set of questions is to listen to other people interacting and asking questions. Write them down and add them to a list in your journal. Some good open-ended questions are: "How is it with your soul?" "What has been going on for you, lately?" "What do you need to grow at this point in your life?" "What has the group meant to you lately?" You will have to come up with questions that are consistent with your personality and things that you are comfortable processing with people.

If you are leading a small group, then you will want to visit with people when they are in another setting. Touch base with them by stopping by their home. Look up a few people each week at church. Go out for coffee. The principle was developed for large corporations where huge segments of a population and multiple business cultures were all contained in one massive complex. You could literally just walk through the place and touch base with huge groups and cross-sections.

I think the best part of this activity comes from collecting images about who the people in your group are in their varied settings. If you are at the office, seeing people at their desk or in their cubicle can reveal some individual tastes and traits you would not normally pick up in a meeting. The same is true of visiting someone in their home. Going out for coffee can relay a whole chunk of personality that is not revealed in the group setting.

> *A leader knows that getting out and about among the people he/she is leading is vital in being able to see them in diverse settings, taking their pulse, checking for needs, and listening to where things are at for people.*

Connectivity Toolbox
—Stuff for your Journal

- Google "Tom Peters MBWA" and read up on the spreading of this leadership principle in the business community during the 1980's as a result of the research he did for *In Search of Excellence*. Write about what you find in your journal and start a discussion with your group about the impressions your members have of this idea. Has anyone read the book? Talk about it if they have.

- Make a list of "listening posts" that you have for each group you are a part of. When you list them in your journal, be sure to identify what group it is, whether you are the leader of the group or not, and the "listening posts" that you have available to you for that group.

- Write a list of open ended questions that you can use to take the pulse of your group. Put this list in your journal. Refer to it often.

- Spend some time talking with Jesus about walking around. Ask Him about how it helped His ministry. Listen for His reply within your heart and record what you hear. Spend some time writing out things you think Jesus accomplished as He walked among the people in their villages and homes.

- Google the article "MBWA After All These Years". It will take you to the dispatch on tompeters.com. Read the article and write down some thoughts to discuss with the group discussing this book. Take the liberty to bounce around the site and see some of the other cool things that are there. Share those things with your group as well..

- Be sure to go to your schedule or calendar and pre-schedule times to mingle among your group. If it requires making "coffee-dates" with folks at Starbucks, get on the phone and do that. Make sure you are hardwiring this idea into your life by planning it into your calendar and keeping it their.

- Workbook pages at: http://feedmysheepleadmysheep.blogspot.com/

31

Servant Leadership

ROBERT K. GREENLEAF WROTE an article on leadership (published in the 1970's) that began a world-wide shift in the way we think about leadership. He challenged traditional models of leadership by suggesting that the role of the servant had a potent energy and power in leading people. The person who served others could truly lead others because they had the best interests of the other in mind. He was clear that it was the servant that leads. The leader could not simply add service to others to their list of things to do. The true leader –according to Greenleaf—is the one with a servant's heart.

Greenleaf took his ideas from a short novel by Herman Hesse entitled, "The Journey East". The main character in the story is a servant that is tending the needs of a group of travelers on their journey. His name is Leo. The whole trip falls apart when Leo slips away from the group. Later in life, one of the travelers runs across Leo and discovers that he had been the head of a secret brotherhood all along and was a master teacher. He was a servant with immense depth.

The notion of a servant leader is not new to the world because of Hesse or Greenleaf. We should clearly recognize its presence in Noah, Moses, Elijah, Jonah, and of course Jesus—as well as countless other men and women of the Judeo-Christian biblical canon. I would like us to take a look at three images of servant-hood that arise surrounding Jesus.

I want to look at Jesus washing the disciples' feet, the woman who anoints Jesus' feet with oil, the Good Shepherd who leaves the ninety-nine to search for the one. These stories carry a picture of serving that reveals its ability to empower, sanctify, and redeem people in and among the lives they live. They are also images of the character of a person; they are things that come out of a person as natural responses to situations. I am not saying that they are not learned traits—they may be. What I am saying is that these types of offerings—the kind the people in these stories make—are examples of who they are as people. They are natural and outward reflections of an interior reality. They are examples of servants who lead, not leaders who serve.

This really gets at the whole notion of this book. Leading is the development of our lives over time; it is the becoming of a person, not just the individual acts of that person. Leading lies on the razor's edge of our identity. A person cannot be a leader a part from his or her own self. The acts of the leader are not leadership itself; they are fruits of leadership. The person is the leader. Leadership goes beyond actions into ways of being.

In the story of Jesus washing the disciples' feet we see the presence of a person as an empowering energy. It was not just the act of washing feet that empowered the disciples with the resources they needed to survive. It was the very person of Jesus—who was always serving them—that edged them closer to God. It was not one act alone, but that one act fit into a whole lifestyle of serving. Nontheless we must build acts of foot-washing into our lives so they may shape us into the people we need to become.

This image reveals to us the true circular nature of our identity as people. We are truly hard-pressed to know whether behavior is innate or learned. What we must do, is stand before the presence of "person" and say yes to both. Personhood and identity are both learned and innate. The serpent is biting its tail. We must allow our identity to come up out of us, but we must also fashion some of what comes up into something else.

When Jesus was teaching the crowds He was washing their feet. When Jesus was healing the sick He was washing their feet. Because He was and is God, everything He did for any of the least of these was done as a servant and as an act of washing their feet. He did not need to do anything that He did because He was God. But, he did all that He did because He was and is a servant. This is how we are to sustain our servant-hood as well. We must let go of any idea that we are better than anyone else. We must serve because it is who we are. If we are not there yet, then we need to get serious about letting Jesus get us to that place from the inside out.

Then there is the story of the woman who washes Jesus' feet with her hair and anoints them with oil. Her act is reprimanded by the do-gooder nature of the disciples. She is made to feel she could have cared for the poor with the money she could have gained from selling the oil instead of wasting it on Jesus' feet. Of course Jesus lets them know they are way off. It is not about the whole outward show of what we do and to whom or for whom. The real drama is what is going on in the heart. When we do any act, it is our heart that determines the nature of that act. It is our heart that sanctifies the actions we perform. If she had despised Jesus in her heart as she anointed His feet, I am sure the story would have taken on a different meaning and ending.

Finally, the story of the shepherd that left the whole flock of sheep to tend to finding and rescuing the one lost sheep reveals that risk for another's well being is at the heart of serving as well. We leave our own comfort of fulfilling our duty as "helpful people" and run the risk of the flock speaking badly of us, or overthrowing our power while we are away, or getting eaten by wolves because we so deeply believe in saving sheep that we are reckless in our serving.

The whole notion of servant leader is just another example of how there can be no set patterns to leading people and feeding people. It takes on a fluid nature when we consider that God will call us to lead and feed His children in ways that require us to turn in to our heart and make choices based on our inner understanding of what it means to bring people to Jesus for His food. We need to stay plugged in to figure this out, because just like the manna, God's offerings appear anew each day. We cannot store up the nourishment He offers.

Many of the traits that Greenleaf identifies as servant qualities are things we have already discussed. But, of the traits there are two that emerge as preeminent. They are the ability to build community and the desire to see others succeed. Bringing people together and helping people advance are what we are doing when we take people to Jesus to feed on Him. Having the heart and mind of a leader enable this growth to happen. They fashion the kingdom of God within us and all around us. Can we get ourselves to the place of Jesus? Can we empty ourselves of who we are and serve others?

> ***A leader struggles and wrestles with the nature of their "person", striving to be pure in the desire to serve others. Being a servant leader is dependent on a heart that is in the battle against self importance.***

Connectivity Toolbox
—Stuff for your Journal

- Google "Servant Leadership and the Individual" by Robert Greenleaf and read this sample of the original article by Greenleaf.
- Write about the key features outlined in this article (in your journal). Discuss this with your group.
- Google "Servant Leadership Theory Carol Smith" and read the article on Greenleaf's theories by Carol Smith.
- Write about the key features outlined in this article (in your journal). Discuss this with your group.
- Google "A Servant Leadership Primer" by Don M. Frick and read the article summation of Servant Leadership.
- Write about the key features outlined in this article (in your journal). Discuss this with your group.
- Keep an ongoing list of servant leader qualities in your journal. Mark off the section with a sticky tab or sheet and add to it as you think of ways to serve or characteristics of servant leadership.
- Pick up a copy of Herman Hesse's short novel: "The Journey East" and read it.
- Discuss the above book with your group that is studying leadership.
- Workbook pages at: http://feedmysheepleadmysheep.blogspot.com/

32

Managing Risk

PEOPLE ARE AFRAID TO talk about risks; they fear that speaking about something "makes it happen". We have mentioned this before. People will "hush" you or "shshshshsh" you if you mention anything that smacks of possible risk, failure, or detriment. If you do not believe me, go ahead and ask—at the next church meeting —what your congregation would do if the building burnt down or if your pastor left the church. Or, you could ask people how they would respond if 60 percent of the congregation left the church and joined with another congregation. I think you know what I am getting at without doing any of those things, but if you do, you are going to get looked at as if you are crazy. You will be told to bite your tongue. People do not like talking about these things because they fear it invites the evil eye.

I think rationally, we all know that this is not true. But, in most cases, we do not go ahead and have the conversations and make the plans to recover from possible disaster. We think it is a waste of time. I might agree with people about it being a waste of time if it were not for November 1979.

I was home from my first trimester away at college. I was getting together with a group of friends at the camp we worked at during summers. We were going to play some football, build a fire, and have some hotdogs and hot chocolate. On the way there, a gasoline tanker truck got stuck on the railroad tracks. Then, with all of the slow-motion of a television drama, the train rounded the bend, heading straight for the truck.

With some inner clarity that came from the routine practice of disaster training at Boy Scouts, I put my car in reverse, backed up—blocking the road with my vehicle—and got out, directing traffic away from the ensuing danger. Within seconds the impact shot gas and an immense subsequent flame all over the road, the tracks and the two transport vehicles. Dozens of people got out of their cars and began wandering in circles, shouting for help and for God. There were police on the other side of the tracks that helped move people out of the wreckage as quickly as they could. Two people died from the fire—the two drivers of the vehicles. I firmly believe the people who could not assist in the crisis were people who never talked about what they would do if a crisis happened. We need to be open enough to talk about the risks we face in life and learn how we could avert them, or respond to them if they are not averted.

Sometimes people of faith fall into the erroneous belief that because they are doing something good that they are immune from bad things happening. All we need do to combat this false belief is remember Job: a man who did everything right in the eyes of God, but still lost everything he had in his life.

Managing our risks as a group and as a leader is about helping people to take a look at the things that could shift in the life of the group and then prepare themselves for that. This must happen on an interior as well as an exterior level. In the groups you lead, have you prepared for what you would do if there was a major storm or any other disaster that could keep you from meeting and gathering? How would you handle the death of one of your members? Or, how about handling a grave illness in one of your members' lives? These are just external shifts.

There are interior shifts as well. How would your group handle it if a member had a nervous breakdown, committed suicide or lost their faith? I am not suggesting that you sit your group down and look at all of these items and then make a plan for them. I think that would require a lot of time and a highly sophisticated group. I am suggesting, however, that you as the leader of the group spend sometime reflecting on these things, planning, and praying about how God would have your respond to some of these issues. They will happen to your group. The longer the group exists, the more likely it is that you will experience one of these things. Bad things happen to good people.

The depth with which you review these issues in and among the group will depend a lot on the role and the function of the group. If you are simply a study group, then you only need to look at things that will affect your group, their study, and the implications of their study in the lives of the individuals in the group. If you are a church steering committee or oversight board, you will need to drill down deeply into the implication of risks and disasters in the overall functioning of your church, its face in the community, and impact in individual congregants' lives. It varies based on the scope of the group you are leading. But, regardless of the scope, you are the one who is going to need to discuss the issues. Other people will be too afraid to discuss them.

> *A leader recognizes that discussing possible risks and disasters in the life of a group does not make them happen. A leader will bring these things up in order to help facilitate familiarity with possible risks and mediate possible solutions and outcomes.*

Connectivity Toolbox
—Stuff for your Journal

- Look up the definition for risk and copy it into your journal.
- Write a list (in your journal) of individual risks you face in life as a professional. What could hurt the work you do as a professional? What keeps you up at night when you think about work? What could cause a severe setback in your workplace?
- Next to each item you list for a risk in the workplace, right a paragraph or two on what you would have to do to avert or recover from the disaster. What would you need to set in place immediately? How would you grow back to the place you had been as a company before the disaster?
- Write an essay in your journal about the things you learned from a disaster in your life. How did it affect you? How did it affect your family? How did it affect others in your life? Did it change the way you live and how did it do that?
- Now, write a list (in your journal) of risks that your group faces on a regular basis (the group studying this handbook). What could possibly interrupt the work that your group is doing?
- Next to each of the risks listed above, write a few paragraphs about what you would have to do to avert or recover from the disaster.
- Google "risk management checklists" and write in your journal about the things you find.
- Write about what risks you face as a follower of Jesus. What threatens your ability to feed on Jesus and lead others to Jesus? Be honest. How about laziness? How about pride? List them all out. Discuss this list with the rest of the group studying this handbook.
- Workbook pages at: http://feedmysheepleadmysheep.blogspot.com/

33

Understanding SWOT

HELPING PEOPLE TO UNDERSTAND the things that impact their life and growth together is essential in leading. It is about turning over the tools of nourishment and development to the whole group so each member can have an equal part in the movement and development of the group. Now, of course, if you live in a dictatorship you will not need to worry about this. But, any leader who recognizes the power of identity and person in development and growth of individuals and groups will be keen on helping people discover the things in their lives that are strengths, weaknesses, opportunities, and threats. It is sets us free.

Most people will recognize "SWOT Analysis" as a business term used in facilitating strategic planning. It is a way of gauging the depth of an organization and taking a panoramic view of the life the group has as a whole and its impact in the world around them. It is no less a tool for individuals and small groups. Knowing your strengths, weaknesses, opportunities, and threats can only increase your self-knowledge and help you grow into the future of your life.

Strengths are things that you do well. These are things that set you apart from other people or other small groups. Some people find it offensive to discuss the things they do well; as if it is somehow prideful. It is not prideful unless you hold it so in your heart. If you are unable to identify what you do well, then you will never be able to step forward and offer that thing when it is needed. If you do not know that you can cook well, then the chances are slim that you will offer your skill when a family in your neighbor needs meals because a fire burned down their home.

Weaknesses are things that your group does not excel in; they are areas you fail in—frequently. They may be internal forces that keep you from success; or external situations you recreate again and again. Think of an old injury and how it impacts things you do. You tend to guard against re-injuring yourself in that area. That tendency toward self-protection is attached to a weakness you have. It is no different with groups. In order to keep them from getting injured again and again in the same way, they need to acknowledge their injuries and weaknesses. Groups need to know how to guard and self-protect. This comes from knowing where the weaknesses are.

Opportunities are things that you can do because you have the strengths you do. If your group gets along really well (a strength), one of your opportunities is to bring other people into the group and include them. This helps to share your strength with others. Opportunities are about sharing your strengths.

Threats are things on the outside of the group that interfere with the groups' ability to do what it does best. They are outside forces that keep you from sharing your strengths. In a business setting we acknowledge competitors as threats and changes in the market as threats. In small groups it can be things that are on your risk list that are the threats. These threats keep the group from interacting with the world around it in a positive fashion.

A lot of leaders do not like to think of small groups or clusters of people with this kind of rigid or analytic view. They do not like to acknowledge that there is a structure underneath all of the positive feeling of groups. These leaders like to pretend that positive things just happen. I am not denying that positive things just happen. But, I am acknowledging that the frequency with which positive things happen in a group is directly related to the groups' ability to identify its strengths, weaknesses, opportunities, and threats and posture themselves in such a fashion as to maximize the use of each in their own growth.

The more you are self-aware, the more you are able to position yourself in places and situations where you will advance and grow. This is at the root of direction and formation. We are directing and forming ourselves toward positive growth in God. We are trying to strive toward becoming deeper and deeper as a person and more and more communal as a group. This can only happen if we have a growing measure of self awareness.

As with all other portions of leadership this functions on the individual and group levels. Individuals in the group need to move toward a clear understanding of their individual SWOT. The group does as well. As a leader, we need to look at our own SWOT and model the behavior that comes from an integrated understanding. We also need to take steps to help the individuals and the group as a whole move in a direction of becoming more self aware. These discussions will feel a lot like peoples' impressions of risk at first. They will fear that talking about things will self-create those things. As they work through these issues with a grounded leader, they will learn that this is not true. Bringing these things into the light can only set us free.

A leader knows that a group can only benefit from a clear and fluid understanding of their strengths, weaknesses, opportunities, and threats as individuals and as a group.

Connectivity Toolbox
—Stuff for your Journal

- Make a list of all your personal strengths in your journal. Then, make a list of all the strengths of your group (discussing this handbook).
- Make a list of all your personal weaknesses in your journal. Then, make a list of all the weaknesses of your group (discussing this handbook).
- Make a list of all your personal opportunities in your journal. Then, make a list of all the opportunities of your group (discussing this handbook).
- Make a list of all your personal threats in your journal. Then, make a list of all the threats of your group (discussing this handbook).
- Discuss the above entries with your group studying this handbook. Write down new ideas that you gained from other peoples entries.
- Google "SWOT in churches" and read two articles in your findings.
- Write a list in your journal of the things you discovered in the above search. Discuss new ideas about SWOT that you found in your reading that you did not discuss in the previous group discussion about SWOT.
- Email the things you found above to the other members of your group that is discussing this handbook. Things that were new ideas since your last group discussion.
- Workbook pages at: http://feedmysheepleadmysheep.blogspot.com/

34

Paying Attention to Space

SPACE OFTEN SEEMS LIKE a minor detail; however, it is not. Space is the springboard for all activity, but it is also a seedbed for individual and group sense of being and identity. The space we meet in shapes the nature and activity of our group. We must pay attention to what that space is imparting and what that space is calling forth from the members who join together within it. Remember, it is the space of your own self that the Holy Spirit chooses to inhabit.

There is no argument when we mention that our homes represent who we are and call us out to become more of who we are. It is no different with the spaces our groups inhabit. There was a classic work by Bruno Bettelheim on the use of space in treatment facilities. It was called "A Home for the Heart". The title itself paints a rich and dappled land scape for the value of place and space in our lives. The places we live and inhabit should somehow represent and call us further into our own hearts.

Think of the feeling of standing in a deep and primeval forest. It calls into our heart and elicits a sense of wonder, awe, and radical amazement. We sense a "hushedness" and "sacredness" to the space. Now think of standing in the center of a shopping mall. It calls forth a completely different set of feelings and responses from within. We no longer have the sense of arboreal antiquity and solemnity. We have a feeling of modern allure and material need. These are whole different sets of interior competencies and qualities. They are shifted and realigned because of the place and space within which we stand.

Groups operate from this same sense of place. We identify with the places we inhabit. We also identify with the people in the space and we reflect what goes on in that space. There is a whole conglomerate of things that get glommed together when we talk about space; the space itself, the people who inhabit the space, and the activities that emerge from the people in the space. Space is rich and dappled.

Think about the space your group inhabits. Does it have its own space? Does it meet in other peoples' space? Does it shift where it meets? How does the shifting reflect the nature of the group? How does the group feel about the space it inhabits? How does the space get a chance to reflect the group that inhabits it? Are there tokens and signs of the groups past growth in the space (i.e., photos of the group, projects from the group, trinkets that express where the group has been). Are there things in the space that call the group to a higher level of being?

We must take active control over our spaces if we wish to have them feed us and nourish us toward the growth we say we aspire to. Simply being passive about the spaces we inhabit in life will set us up to be passive about life itself. Jesus was not passive about space. He wandered Himself into spaces that other people would not be seen in. Why did he do that? He did that because He was not afraid to go places where people were open to God, people that were not hiding behind wealth, pride, and religiosity. He went into socially unacceptable places because that is what the kingdom is all about. He had the Upper Room, but He had the desert, too. He had the home of Mary and Martha, but He had Zacchaeus's place, too.

We should sense a polarity in this understanding. On one hand we need places to go to in order to find solace, comfort, and our center. But, we must also go outside of these places to find the lost and scattered places of the empire where people are hungry beyond belief for God and His Presence. It is not the case of an either or. It is a case of both and. We need places to build interior comfort and peace. We need places that tear us apart and stretch us.

How does your group give space for the prophetic call of Jesus to care for the dispossessed and abandoned? How does your group stretch itself outside and beyond its sense of comfort and personal retreat? We must look to both poles. Space is a place to go into to find rest and repair. Space is also a place we are called out of; called into new and expansive activities that draw us out of our comfort zone and into the ragged edges of God's kingdom. Both of these poles are a part of the journey.

It is curious that the church as an historic body has done one or the other well, but for the most part not been able to pull of doing both of these things well. Sure, in the medieval period we had luxurious palace churches and an extensive missionary outreach at the same time, but the outreach was the Crusades and the palace churches were built on the backs of the poor. I am not sure that qualifies as doing both well. It seems a bit ethically askew.

Is there a way for people to honor space for meeting and housing the spirit of their soul and at the same time to step out of that space and into the challenge and abandonment of the wilderness of life? Are we able to retreat and go forth? Is it possible to expand and contract? Can we do both without sacrificing either? I believe we can. We must bring this to the surface of our consciousness, though, if we expect to engage and win in the struggle.

At the core of this image and discussion is the simple reality that groups are called to be for themselves—to help each other grow and mend in the grace and peace of Jesus. But, they are also called to be for others—to bring the comfortable terror of the Gospel into the lives of all people who are hungering for it. The image of feeding and leading is again central. Feeding goes on in spaces where the followers gather to connect with Jesus. Leading goes on in areas where people are hearing about how the hunger deep down in their soul-lives is really a hunger for feeding on Jesus.

> *Leaders challenge their groups to find spaces and places that allow them to retreat, relax, and to repair. They also know how to challenge their groups to leave their comfort zone and go out into new-growth-places; places where other people need them to be.*

Connectivity Toolbox
—Stuff for your Journal

- In your journal, write a description of the space your group is meeting in to discuss this book.

- In your journal, describe how the space your group is meeting in to discuss this book is reflective of the group and what it does, or is not reflective of the group and what it does?

- In your journal, list the things you believe should be in the space your group meets to discuss this book. Share those things together with the other members of this group.

- Visit "The Monadnock Institute" website at: http://www.franklin-pierce.edu/institutes/monadnockinst/index.htm Wander through the site and make some observation in your journal about what this site mentions in regard to the power of space to identify and inform culture. Discuss with your group how this impacts leadership.

- Imagine you had the opportunity to create whatever space you could or would want for your group that is meeting to discuss this book. What would you create? Where would it be? Draw it and describe it in detail in your journal.

- Share what you have written and drawn in the exercise above with the group. How does your image of space for the group help develop and inform your sense of leadership? Discuss this at length.

- Make a list of all the places you inhabit during the course of a week: home, church, work, etc.. Next to the list, in your journal, put an "x" next to all of the spaces you inhabit that you think are doing a fair job of representing and informing the groups that inhabit them.

- How often does your group leave the comfort of its space to bring the power of the Gospel to those who do not yet know what it is they are hungering for? Discuss this amongst yourselves. Make a plan.

- Workbook pages at: http://feedmysheepleadmysheep.blogspot.com/

35

Working With and As a Team

EVERYONE VIEWS THEMSELVES AS a team player because we esteem this quality. It is something we look up to and hold our groups to in order to acknowledge their successfulness as a group. A team is a group that works well. Not all groups are able to get themselves to the place of being a team, but a lot of them believe they have. Every team is a group, but not every group is a team.

"Teammanship" is the ability of a member of a group to work toward a whole that is larger than him/herself. It is a yielding over to the higher good of the group by an individual in the group. Working as a team is more all encompassing than that. Working as a team is not only an individual yielding over to the higher good of the group by each individual in the group; it is also the setting up of an ongoing process whereby the whole group is continually about weeding out things that work against a unified presence of the group. It is growing into becoming a team in every aspect of the life of the group. It is "teamship".

This sense of "teamship" is an organic process that takes over once each individual has given up their life to the group. It is a process that we do well at and a process that we fail at. We grow in and out of our abilities to live and grow as a team. Sometimes a group is a team acclimated toward a common goal and a common end. Other times a group is a bunch of individuals clamoring to have their own needs met. A skillful leader can clearly communicate to a group where they are on the "teamship" continuum and call them to a place they would do well to attain to.

Working with and as a team has many implications. It involves remembering that there are more than one possible belief, option, outcome, feeling, skill, and desire to each and every thing that exists within the life of a group of people. Each individual in the group brings a whole sense of these things to the group. Moving from being a group to being a team involves the development of processes and events that honor the individual sense of identity in a way that allows for a surrendering of individual identity into a larger unified identity that represents the group as a whole. This consensual blending and melding of the one into the many tends to be centered on specifically chosen modes of being or focuses as a group. It is done with the development of the team in mind.

I want to back out of this conversation for a moment and make an observation. A lot of times when a leader is helping to facilitate the development of a group into a team it is at the behest of his/her own personal desires or whims for the group. The leader is really manipulating the group into accomplishing his/her agenda. I mention this because it is a part of the process of a group becoming a team to be able to recognize this phase of group development and to do the hard work of challenging the leader and the group to do a better job of representing the whole and not just the leader.

Yes, it is a lot more work and it takes a lot longer to get to this place, but it is really more communal. A leader is a facilitator of freedom. This means helping to reveal all of the options and constructively aiding the process of consensus—not rallying the group behind our own aims as a leader. The development of a group into a team requires sacrifice.

The development of a group into a team requires compromise. There can be no shortcut. So, if you believe your group is a team and you have not gone through the hard work of rising out of your conflicts to the unified field above them, then you are really only a pseudo-team. You may be on the road to becoming a team, but you are not there yet.

I believe every group is always in the battle of becoming or not becoming a team. I believe the ebb and flow of becoming or not becoming a team is the ongoing tension that exists in the group. I believe it will be a lifelong goal of any group. I believe we will have glimpses of being a team, but that most of the time we will be a group of individuals. This is the razor's edge of being a group. This is the edge where failure should teach us how to grow. When a group has functioned as a team, they know it, they feel it, and they are nourished by it.

Being a team requires some small skills. We need to be able to accept and work with criticism. We need to be able to decide on common directions that will benefit the group as a whole—bringing the group further ahead on its development as a unit. We need to be able to see how laying aside individual wants can stimulate growth in the whole group—the unit. We will need to be able to listen deeply to what people are saying and be able to reframe this data into statements that make sense to and for the whole group, not just each member of the group. We need to be able to build consensus by sharing common ground.

This requires pointing out where common ground exists. It means being able to provide space for group members to challenge each other with engaging dialogue—making mistakes and finding ways to improve on those mistakes as time goes by. Ultimately, becoming a team will require the leader to lay aside their role as facilitator and take up the role of "one among many". This final notion is what often keeps groups just on this side of becoming a team. Leaders often stifle team development; they develop clubs instead.

> *A leader recognizes how each of the individual component members of a group fits together into the whole of the group. The leader challenges the members of the group to see these same things and work toward being a genuine team—a community of equals—by rising above the conflicts and needs of the individual and growing toward a unified end.*

Connectivity Toolbox
—Stuff for your Journal

- How do you feel your group is at being a team?
- List things your group has done which you feel show a "unified group"—one that functioned as a team (in your journal). Share these things with the group.
- Write about (in your journal) the differences between being a club and being a team. Write about the differences between being a group and a team.
- Google "images for teamwork". Print out 5—10 of the images and bring them to the group studying this book. Discuss the implications and meanings behind the images the members of the group selected. Choose one image that the group can agree on that will become an image for teamwork for your group.
- Write an article on teamwork. Share it with your group.
- Have the group collect all of the articles on teamwork written by the group members. Publish them in a newsletter for the entire congregation of your church or parent organization. Share it with friends and family as well.
- Ask for feedback about your teamwork articles.
- Collect all of the feedback about your teamwork newsletter and discuss it as a group.
- On a scale of one to ten (ten being the BEST), how does this group function as a team?
- List five things in your journal you could do to help improve your groups' functioning as a team. What things could the group do to help improve its functioning as a team?
- Workbook pages at: http://feedmysheepleadmysheep.blogspot.com/

36

Time Management

Improving the use of time as an individual and as a group is something we will most likely be doing in all stages and phases of development. Whether we are trying to get more work done in an allotted time frame or are trying to re-balance our down-time; managing what we do, when we do it, and how we do it will always be something we strive to improve. Time is a limited commodity. We cannot regain lost time. We cannot cram more time into the now. We cannot buy more time for the future. It is out of our hands to do anything about time except manage the way we use it.

Everything that goes on in the life of an individual or a group is vying for our time. Each new variable in our lives and each new member in our groups will often disrupt and reroute the way we use time. These changes may cause us to inadvertently hit the reset button—losing the skill we had developed until this point. We go back to the bottom and start over again. It is not unusual to go through periods of having to relearn time management skills and principles. That is why it is good to acknowledge that it will be something we always strive to improve.

There are a couple of tools that we need to hardwire into our personality and use in our person on a regular basis to make time management rich and productive for us. First, we need to carry a pad of paper and a pencil everywhere we go—particularly to meetings. We need to be prepared. If we do not have some place to take the abstract ideas, words, and timeframes about things and symbolically mark down each portion on paper, we will forget all of the components, intricacies, and minutia of what we are working on and we will have to revisit the conversation later when we realize that something is missing. Going back to something that has been previously discussed or worked on is a big waste of time. I think people would be surprised the amount of time they spend repeating tasks that should not have been repeated. These are unnecessary redundancies. It is also not as easy to recreate past meetings and events as we might think. Write things down so you do not need to backtrack. Backtracking is an unnecessary redundancy. Removing unnecessary redundancies is a good thing to do.

A second rudimentary task in time management is making sure you hardwire things immediately into your systems—personal and group. If you are planning a get-together to further discuss one of the sections of the book, it should be instantly (while in the meeting) posted to a digital calendar somewhere, or on a wall calendar, or in a personal planning book. This saves time of having to do it later and keeps from using too much brain space for random and nonessential data. If you do not have a calendar or planner of some kind with you, get one. But, in the meantime go ahead and jot it down on your pad of paper. The goal is to remove unnecessary redundancies. And, if you are the person in the group that needs to contact the group to remind them about these events, you should write down in your calendar—right then and there—what day you need to send out the reminder.

A third rudimentary task is to assign weight to the work. This means adding goals and priorities (smaller bite-sized tasks for each goal under each goal) to the things you are writing down or planning. Make sure that your lists and calendars are composed of clear goals, tangible priorities, and rank ordered dependencies. Making diagrams or mind maps can be a helpful way of organizing concepts into goals and weighted priorities.

If you keep these three rudimentary tasks in your daily routine, you will automatically be light years ahead of most people. You will also be modeling some essential behaviors to those around you. I have been to meetings with key leaders of large organizations that have not brought with them any paper, pencil, or planner. Sometimes—even when people have a way to record data—people will sit through a meeting without taking a single note.

Doing these three things will help to conclude and close out planning functions so you can move on into the work you need to do—the actual execution phase. These ancillary planning steps are meant to be finished at the meeting. A lot of people carry them with them to do later, which eventually eats into the time they need to get the actual work done that has been planned (execution). If you do all of your recording, weighing, scheduling tasks while you are with the group deciding on these things, then you will not need to sit in your car or at your desk later and recreate the whole process. You have that time to get to work on your assignments or to do something else.

I have a pretty good memory, but I learned long ago that when I am engaged in a multilayered conversation I may forget the sequence of events or goals if I do not write them down. I write things down and I mark sequences and priorities right into the list at the outset. The act of writing things down is itself an aid to memory. It is as if you have heard the information two times; first, in the oral discussion, second, in the echoing of the words as you write them down.

Even if you have a steel trap for a brain, as a leader you need to write things down. A good leader recognizes that taking notes is an excellent practice and it models critical behaviors. A lot of times leaders think of themselves as "above the need to take notes"; that they are the idea engines of the group and the other people are the grunt workers. "Let them take the notes," they think. It is not about the image people have of us that is important. It is what we choose to model that is important. If we do not write things down, we are telling everyone else in the group that they do not need to write things down. We are also telling them that we are trying to appear aloof and superior in our posturing—that we are somehow above or beyond the need to take notes. This is a bad image to pose and certainly against the way of the heart.

In addition to these simple features of time management, it is also important to verbally identify when we are busy, have time constraints, or are unavailable. Keeping this information from people is not helpful. We must learn to communicate these things so people have an adequate understanding of other mitigating forces that drive our use of time. We all have limits and communicating our limits is crucial in modeling behavior; it is also crucial in maintaining a balanced life and an ability to successfully meet deadlines and commitments. People that do not set and communicate limits are people who do not have a realistic view of themselves and the things they are capable of. So, as leaders we must reveal our limitations.

It is also important to make sure that we communicate the structure behind scheduled events. This means meetings should always have a written agenda. If the agenda is always the same, then a poster can be printed, laminated and hung on the wall or we can hand out agenda sheets. If we are trying to be eco-friendly then a whiteboard can be posted with the agenda on it for everyone to see.

Even if we are having bible study we should have a format and an agenda. It keeps goals, tasks, and structure before our eyes. It is a good idea to make margin notes about time frames so people get the idea that things need to move along. If we want to have a one hour total study and we need to have prayer first and then snacks afterward (within that hour timeframe), we need to lay out an agenda with allotted times next to each portion of that agenda.

All of this does not mean that we cannot extend schedules and break formatted structures. But, we need to have a place to begin. Having these things available for people gives an opportunity toward focus. Without these tools groups are not forced to face the tough challenges that time presents to us. Time is limited in life. We cannot get it back, and we cannot purchase more of it. The time we spend with groups of people and by ourselves is a small reminder of the finite nature of time itself. Learning to orchestrate its use and celebration in groups can feed the ability to do the same in our individual lives as well.

> *Leaders recognize the value of time and utilize tools and techniques to focus the group's interaction with and throughout time. Lack of structure can be detrimental to group and individual development as well as a robust understanding of time management. Leaders also recognize when to go off-grid or off-schedule and "waste time" having fun and connecting in non-linear way*

Connectivity Toolbox
—Stuff for your Journal

- Go to: http://downloads.cas.psu.edu/leadership/pdf/timemngm brochure.pdf online and read each of the three time management brochures posted. (Or, surf the web for some other data on time management activities.) Print them out and take them to your next group meeting (of those discussing this handbook). Review them together, pausing to discuss new ideas. Make sure to make notes in your journal of tips you find in the group setting.

- Go to: http://www.mindtools.com/pages/article/newISS_01.htm Read up on how to create mind maps. Watch the video. (Or, surf the web for some other articles on mind mapping.) Print out the material and be sure you understand the key concepts and the procedures for making a mind map.

- Make a mind-map in your journal about some upcoming project, trip, or other activity that you will be participating in. Be sure to use ample colors and logos or images to help facilitate understanding the map. Share this map with the others in your group that is discussing this handbook.

- In your journal draw out a schedule for your ideal or perfect week. Be creative and make it suit your personality. Include all of the things that you would like to or hope to have accomplished by the end of that week. Make sure you include work, home, personal, and social activities. If you need an idea to model your ideal week on, take a look at Michael Hyatt's leadership blog at: http://michaelhyatt.com/ and search for HOW TO BETTER CONTROL YOUR TIME BY DESIGNING YOUR IDEAL WEEK.

- Write about (in your journal) areas you feel you are not doing a good job in managing your time. Make sure you look at areas that are related to work, family, social activity, personal time, and faith. What might you do to help yourself manage your time better in these areas?

- What is the biggest waste of time you experience in church groups and your faith based communities? Talk about these with your group studying this handbook.
- Workbook pages at: http://feedmysheepleadmysheep.blogspot.com/

37

Interpersonal Relationships

INTERPERSONAL RELATIONSHIPS ARE ABOUT how we connect with people. In the group setting we connect with everyone else in the group as individuals and also in small subsets, cliques, and gatherings within the overall group. There are interactions that will only happen between you and certain people in the group simply because other people in the group do not share that level of relationship with you. This layered approach to connections within the group is deeply complex and adds dimensions to group dynamics that people often forget about. A good leader is conscious of this multi-dimensioned matrix that exists invisibly in groups based on relationships. Just like making a good soup, we must be aware—as leaders—of the ingredients added to the pot and how they will affect the taste, layers, and texture of the soup (the swirling soup of relationships).

There are many ways to view how the leader fits into the group in order to be the best leader they can be. I am a firm believer in the leader being a member of the group with facilitating capabilities and responsibilities. That is, I think the leader needs to put him/herself out there and risk like and with everyone else in the group. On top of this the leader is responsible for seeing to the overall flow and function of the group. It is a lot of work, but the "detached leader model" really does not do justice to group growth or leadership.

The leader really must function on both levels. In fact, when they do, they are modeling a whole new paradigm for leadership; one that will live on into the future with much deeper roots. The leader is not some Freudian Therapist, monitoring the rats in the maze (although some leaders act like it). The leader is a member of the group who believes in the work that the group is doing and participates in that work. The leader also helps to see that the work is carried on into the future.

This poses some real difficulty for some people. Many leaders will holler about the fact that they need to remain professionally aloof or at a distance. I think what these people are really saying is that people need to be careful of how much of themselves they share. I agree with that, but what I think really needs to be communicated around this issue of boundaries is that everyone in the group needs to be aware of and protective of their individual boundaries—not just the leader. People need to be careful with what and how they risk. That goes for all members of the group, though and not simply the leadership.

I think what has happened in the past is that leaders—particularly in therapeutic environments—have isolated themselves from the process of the group and have drawn out the vulnerability of the group members so as to make them unduly exposed in the group; they act like the lifeguard of the process of the group. This gives the leader a magical sense of power over the group which I believe is wrong. It also fails to relay to the group that the leader is just as broken as the rest of them. This has set leaders and clergy on pedestals that are not only inappropriate, but unattainable. This can only lead to an idolatry based on misconception and an inevitable collapse that will take people by surprise. We have all seen this happen.

Although there will be times when dealing with specific things that the leader will need the perspective and advantage of the lifeguard stand, we must remember that it is a function that other members of the group may be called to at other times in the development of the group. A leader knows when others are better suited for and even called into roles and functions within the growth of the group because they are in a better place to perform that role or function. A leader senses when the Spirit of God is calling someone else to the lifeguard stand to take over the role and function—even if it is for just one single instance. A leader is also able to confess when they have failed in this task, and change their behavior accordingly.

There is a root premise here that I think we have left out of our discussion of leadership in the churches over the years. The premise is that the role and function of leadership is a ministry of calling. That is, the Holy Spirit calls men and women to lead. Because it is a ministry of calling, the leadership may shift and change over time as God calls other people into positions to facilitate growth. What we have done in the church since the beginning is to see that people that are called to lead are set up in lifelong vocations of leadership in the church.

We have done this because it was how Imperial positions of leadership in the Empire (Greco-Roman at the time of Christ) were filled. We also did it because it was easier to make these changes in positions less frequently. Keeping people in fixed roles for longer amounts of time helps people know how to navigate among the shoals of power.

There is a whole cascading phenomenon in leadership when we keep positions fixed and develop a sense of promotion based on time served. What ends up happening is an ominous amalgam of power issues that cause all sorts of intrigue and scandal and force people to blackmail one another into staying where they are for security sake.

When we do not take the time to ask the Spirit of God what is required, and then wait for an answer, we jeopardize the growth of the group. It would take us a lot more effort to discern the will of the Spirit on a more regular basis. I am not so sure people believe in God that much that they could trust learning to listen at this level. It is a difficult thing to allow God to structure our leadership and the relationships we encounter.

We would have to really stay connected to God to allow leadership roles to remain that fluid. But look at how hideous things have become because of the way we have chosen to do leadership. Can we really say that the way we do leadership now is a good thing?

When we start talking about interpersonal relationships in the group, we must also keep in mind that there are some usual suspects in groups that we must all learn to relate to. I am not going to list all the types here and now, but you need to explore the possibilities more fully on your own. Here are two.

Every group will have in it one or two people who play the role of Judas. They look like they are your friend, they look like they are a part of the group, but at some critical juncture they will sell you out. These people are here for us to work with. They are here to teach us about not getting attached to the idea of being worshipped and idolized. Their role performs a wonderful function for leaders to hold on to. The Judas in the group is just wearing off the rough edges of our pride. But, we have got to learn how to talk to them, work with them, and facilitate their growth, too. They will draw us out of ourselves into the fields of vulnerability.

There are also Pharisees. These folks will be the power people in the group. They love control, they love force, and they love being elevated above the masses. These folks are also here to keep us humble. But, we will find that they call forth a need for us to turn over their tables of elitism. We will need to safeguard the underdog when it comes to the Pharisees. We will need to defend the cause of the widow and orphan in their presence. They will also draw us out of ourselves into the fields of vulnerability.

Do you see why it was easier to just put people in positions of leadership and leave them there forever? Leadership is a lot of work. It is an ongoing process of the "development of" the person and a "listening to" and "for" the call of the Holy Spirit. It is a "remaining open". That kind of openness is very hard to live on a daily basis. It is easier to hide behind that snowballing amalgam of power and position; ruling like an emperor with an iron fist. It is easier to remove your person from the group itself and act as someone above the group. We are not called to the easy way. Leading and feeding is consuming.

Interpersonal relationships can help us keep a more even keel in church development; in group and individual development as well. It requires that we challenge the ideas of "lifelong leadership", of "leading from above", and of leaders not participating in the groups they lead. If we continue to lead stoically as if we were disembodied spirits or somehow better than the people of God, then we will never understand the true depth of our calling to lead. Our calling to lead is here to teach us that we are broken. And, it is here to teach us that even though we are broken, we can fulfill the work of God. It is here to model that to the other broken people in our lives; the ones God has called us to play the role for.

Leaders recognize that they are a part of the groups they lead. Leaders are not above the groups, but are members of the groups, called by God to reveal the paradox of the Paschal Mystery—we are broken but used by God.

Connectivity Toolbox
—Stuff for your Journal

- Google "group dynamics" and spend some time looking over some of the sites you discover. Jot down some notes in your journal about what you find. Share these observations with your group that is discussing this handbook.

- Write about the people in all of the groups you belong to which you have the hardest time getting along with. What is it about these people that you have the hardest time with? What have these people taught you about yourself? What do you think these people are trying to express in your encounters?

- Pray for all of the people you listed in your journal in the above exercise. Ask for a heart that is able to understand who they are and where they have come from. Pray for their growth.

- Write a letter to an imaginary young man or woman (in your journal) that you are trying to mentor in leadership. Make sure you expound to them what you think leadership is, how you can discern a call to leadership, and the key features that you believe are present in the heart and mind of a person who is called to lead. Share with them a few examples of things you have been through yourself in leading others. Go ahead and make it sound like an Epistle that you are writing to set this young person on a noble and worthy path toward Jesus.

- Think about the groups you are leading. Begin to pray about them members of the group and discern if there are people in the group that may be ready to help facilitate some of the work. Be serious in your discernment process to discover if God is asking you to open up the future of the group's growth by allowing others to bring their witness into the facilitating of the group. Be sure to add this process to your group calendar a couple of times a year—so you do not forget to do it again.

- Workbook pages at: http://feedmysheepleadmysheep.blogspot.com/

38

Problem Solving

PROBLEM SOLVING IS PUTTING the pieces together. It is using all of our ingenuity, creativity, and imagination to figure out where this piece goes and what piece may or may not fit next to it. It is the art of putting together a puzzle, doing a word search, or unscrambling letters into phrases. In fact, puzzles are really a playful means of problem solving. They are warm up exercises for the problem solving brain.

When we step into the role or mindset of problem solving, we are entering into a state in which we would do well to accept the ideas of trial and error, successes and failures. Problem solving is a stage in the development of how and what we will put into practice—the how and what of execution. It helps if we take a recreational or light-hearted posture when we participate in problem solving activities.

Think of standing over a picture puzzle. There are many ways to begin the process. Some people look for all of the straight edge pieces and try to make sense of how they all fit together to form a frame. Or, how about a word puzzle, when we begin these, some people will go through the clues one after another and start by filling in all of the answers that they know without having to think too hard. In either example people then go back and begin a second level of play, a second level to the process. And so it goes, on and on like this in layers: some pieces here; some words there. We do this until we have completed the puzzle.

Solving problems is no different. We have a beginning to the process and then layer after layer until we have solved or finished with the problem. It is important to figure out how to begin the process of solving problems. Some people rely on making a mind map to get the creative juices flowing. They write out the problem in the center of the page; placing a circle or a square around the problem. Then they draw spider-like legs, radiating out from the center. Each leg has a bubble attached to it. In that bubble or "call-out" they would write something that is associated with the problem. Then, each of these would have spider-like legs radiating off of them. At the end of these legs would be solutions to each of the associated images of the problem. On and on this goes until there seems to be enough data to begin execution.

Other people will do brainstorming, affinity diagrams, or lists of pros and cons. It does not matter which technique we select, what matters is that we approach the solution process with a free association and open minded sort of posture or mindset. We are collecting mass quantities of data at the outset and then slowly weeding it out or whittling it down until we see how and where pieces may come together.

In problem solving, unlike in doing puzzles, we will actually throw out pieces that do not belong to the picture. Think of it in terms of erasing a wrong answer in a crossword puzzle. This flexible give and take of successes and failures produces an energy that drives the process forward: erasing old words we find new words to go in their place.

Some leaders try to overstep their bounds in these problem solving processes. We must really see ourselves as members of the group in these instances. We do well to offer solutions like the rest of the group, but we should also encourage others to offer contradictory reality (ie, "that is the wrong word" or, "that does not fit there") in the process; rather than us being the person who always judges toward accuracy and correctness. This judging toward accuracy and correctness is a part of the process, but eliciting this oversight function from others in the group strengthens the cohesion and facilitates a more robust modeling of leadership.

When we are in positions of needing to solve problems, it is advisable to let other members of the group facilitate the recording of the suggestions, or the overall flow of the process. It spreads the leadership out and it gives ample space for practicing new leadership techniques within the safety of a previously established and engaged group of people. This makes it less threatening. This will assure that there is one person in the group you can all compare your notes with. These processes are quite busy and confusing; you will all want to be on the same page at the end. Having an anchor notetaker you can compare with will help you stay aligned.

There is an overall flow to the process that we need to keep in mind. We are moving from the beginning of the process where we identify and define the problem; to the end of the process where we execute our solutions. In the middle we are listing possible solutions and judging which of them will be more or less effective in ameliorating the problem at hand. Because it is a process, we may erase things and go back to the beginning anywhere along the work. At some point, we need to wrap up and decide that we are willing to go ahead and execute the solutions we have developed. Built into the discussion should be the fact that if these do not work, we simply return to the beginning again and have another go at it.

This type of work will show people that trial and error is really a creative process. Solving problems is something that can feed us at a deep level as we begin to notice that there are many options in figuring out how to live life. The erratic nature of coming up with a series of associations and solutions stimulates neural development and it enhances our ability to cope.

> *A leader recognizes the value of free association in the process of coming to terms with problem solving. A leader will allow the entire group to move the problem solving process along its course from inception to execution.*

Connectivity Toolbox
—Stuff for your Journal

- Google "problem solving techniques" and list out in your journal all of the ideas you find there. Put an "x" next to ones you have utilized in the past. Talk about—with your group studying this handbook—new or novel ideas you found in this search.
- Google "problem solving techniques at mind tools" or go directly to the www.mindtools.com website and search for problem solving. Read the material on this site for problem solving.
- List the four steps to problem solving that are posted on the www.mindtools.com website—in your journal. Or, search for other steps and stages to problem solving and record these in your journal. Discuss them with your group.
- Develop a make-believe problem and go through a solving process with the group you are studying this handbook with. Log your process in your journal.
- Draw a mind map in your journal that is an image of a personal problem you are working on. Use the diagram to help you plan and plot out a solution to execute.
- Write about—in your journal—how the problem solving mind map you did above was either a success or failure when you implemented and executed your solution. Would you do this again?
- Write out a few paragraphs—in your journal—about how your groups (any groups you are involved in or lead) do at problem solving. Does the process flow naturally? Are they effective? Do they need a lot more work? What could help them get better at the process?
- Workbook pages at: http://feedmysheepleadmysheep.blogspot.com/

39

Integrity

INTEGRITY IS A CONSISTENT soundness throughout. If we are talking about a clay pot, it is a clay pot that has no air bubbles or imperfections in the clay walls. The uniformity of the thickness and purity is even throughout. If we are talking about a person or a group with integrity it is the same. Our integrity is about being consistent in all aspects of our being—"throughout". Obviously we do not get there overnight. Integrity is a quality that we develop over time; and in many cases, the older we become the more we recognize the value of such a quality.

When we are younger we are often more naïve and less likely to use a rich and robust quality control process or scrutinization in living and building our lives. As we get older we tend to notice that when something is consistent throughout—like that clay pot—we can trust it more and over a longer period of time. We also notice that when something lacks integrity, it falls apart or crumbles much more quickly. We get picky about the things we like because we tire of connecting to things that are not consistent or fall apart too quickly.

If we build a log cabin and do not find logs that are consistently sound throughout, then we may be faced with an expedited rotting or decaying process. Some logs may become soft in the middle before others. So, when building a life or a group of lives, like building a log cabin, we look for a consistent soundness throughout.

The process of time and scrutiny can help us to correct areas that are not consistent. We can add more clay to thicken the weaknesses in the walls of the clay pot of life. Thinking about this in terms of our abilities to lead, we must recognize that our ongoing connection to Jesus and our growth and deepening as a person is all about the shoring up of who we are. As we take on more and more of the divine nature (which is imparted to us by grace) we become more and more like Jesus. Jesus is the richest model of integrity that we can identify with.

On the Christian journey we are called to become more and more transformed into the image and likeness of Jesus. If we consider the "image" of Jesus to be the overall structure of the log cabin we spoke of in the above example—the projected blueprint and plans, then the "likeness" of Jesus would be using the same materials to build that log cabin as Jesus used. The log cabin of our lives is to be built with the same plans used in building Jesus (image) and our materials (likeness) of love, joy, peace, patience, etc. are to be materials with high integrity (consistent throughout). We are to work with God in the process of God's building us into the image and likeness of the God-Man. We are to become by grace what He is by nature. Our integrity as individuals and groups (in the church) is based on becoming the image and likeness of Jesus.

There is a radical departure here—in what I am about to say—from some of our previous images and pictures for what it means to be formed and directed into the image and likeness. As we are growing into the image and likeness we will find areas of our lives in which the integrity of our walls is not what it should be. We actually need to replace broken portions of our lives (this is what forgiveness and grace are all about) with new, stronger, and healed pieces. We are a composite of rebuilt pieces of our own selves.

We should find some hope in the fact that a broken bone can become as good as new after the healing process runs its course. We can replenish and refresh the portions of our lives that fall apart and decay. We can be made "new" as the Christian faith teaches: born again. Our hope is in the power and love of God: Father, Son, and Holy Spirit.

The Trinity is a keen example of integrity. There is a sameness and continuity through the Godhead in its Essence. The Essence of God is a consistent soundness throughout its reality of Trinity. The Godhead is not thinner or thicker in the Son, than it is in the Father or the Spirit. This is what Jesus was talking about when He said that when any man sees Him they have seen the Father that sent Him. By inclusion then, this is also true when we are speaking of the Holy Spirit of God.

Leaning into our growth and sanctification in the spiritual life, we uncover the fact that we are called into becoming more and more like Christ. We become by grace, what He is by nature. This is an integrating of the Godhead into our lives. I will not speak here about how that happens, but it is the beginning of a deepening journey (albeit one fraught with potential risk and misunderstanding—what the church has called heresy) in which we are refashioned into the likeness of Jesus. The integrating of our lives into the Godhead is the converse side of the story.

This knitting together of God and man is the spiritual journey. Integrating more and more of God into our lives is how we are able to envelop a divine integrity. It is possible in the sanctification of our lives. We are built into the Dwelling Place of the Most High God. Herein is our basis for integrity.

> *The leader recognizes that integrity in life comes from a process of being remade by God into the image and likeness of Jesus. This image and likeness is consistent with the character of God in as much as we allow God to remake us over into His Dwelling Place.*

Connectivity Toolbox
—Stuff for your Journal

- Write in your journal about the integrity in your life of being like Jesus. In what ways do you see you have been changed into the image and likeness of Jesus? In what ways do you still need the redemptive and sanctifying work of the Holy Spirit?

- Make a list (in your journal) of things in your life you depend on to be consistent throughout. What things are you relying on to be of high integrity? Things like the foundation of your home, the stairs, and your relationship with your spouse. How about in your groups? What things do you depend on there to be of high integrity?

- Google "testing for integrity". After reading through several sites, make a list in your journal of ways in which you can test for integrity in things in life. Expound on how you may test for integrity in your own life.

- How is the refining process like integrity? Does suffering play a role in our integrity? How does it do that? Discuss these things as a group and be sure to journal out any of the ideas that impact you during the discussion.

- Integrity is about quality. Make a list in your journal of personal traits and characteristics that reveal the presence of integrity in the life of Jesus. This should be as full a list as you can write. Include some of the things you wrote in the above exercises, but expand on these notions.

- How do you integrate a thing in your life? Think about that. How do you bring some new thing into your life and make it a part of you? Write that out in your journal.

- Workbook pages at: http://feedmysheepleadmysheep.blogspot.com/

40

Decision Making

Decision making is the stepping out—in one direction or another—into the execution of some form of activity. We collect data, we organize it; using it to feed our concepts, potential directions, and possible solutions. Then, we muster all our effort and make a decision about how, when, where, why, what and if we will execute some activity and move forward (hopefully) toward our goal. Making a decision can often be so overwhelming that people freeze—stopping dead in their tracks. We know that people not only fight or take to flight when deciding how to deal with some obstacle or stressor; they can freeze as well.

Fight, flight, or freezing tends to be a survival mechanism that is triggered by a sense of imminent danger. It comes from the feeling that there is something we should fear on our horizon. It does not mean that we will necessarily move into fear, it just means that our systems senses a threat and we are leaping into a mode that will process that threat, determine its level, and then choose a course of action. That is of course if all the pistons are firing properly. When we are compromised or in conflict, we are not functioning the way we normally do and the need to choose may not produce the same response now as it did at some other point in life.

There is also a splitting of hairs that goes on in the decision making process. While making a decision does mean leaning into that decision in such a way as to begin the execution of what it is we have decided on, the making of the decision does not mean that the execution will be followed up on in some regular amount of time. We can decide today, but take the execution no further until a month from now. Some people even make a decision and then freeze, fight, or head into flight; going no further into the execution of the plan. Although the decision making process is a part of execution, many people decide and then go no further.

When this happens, it makes me wonder if the person has made the wrong decision. Or, perhaps they were really only making a decision to please someone or meet a deadline. It is a decision with hesitancy.

When we look at the decisions we make in terms of how they affect the operation of the rest of our lives, I think we need to talk about things like momentum and impact. The decisions we make will impact every other area of our lives. In fact, the impact may be so immense that we may slow down or even stop all together the forward motion—or momentum—of our lives. It may also be the case that the decisions we make may encourage or foster the momentum in our lives.

I am pretty sure people do not think about this when making most decisions. I am willing to bet that most decisions are made from a gut or feeling level. This is clearly important in the mix, but it should not be the sole impetus for making a decision. This is another area where we can see that leadership is a blending of traits and characteristics. In this instance we can easily imagine that taking the vantage point of surveillance could help us make more accurate decisions the first time. Innovation and circumambulation are helpful in integrating the array of options in a decision making process.

Regardless of which other techniques you bring to bear in the decision making process you had better plan to address fears and risks at the outset. Get them up on the table and discuss them as a part of the overall assessment of things that come to bear on this decision. Be sure to clearly address how you will deal with those concerns that people have that are connected to those fears and risks. If you do not address them, you can be sure that either the people who hold those fears within or the very fears themselves will rear their ugly head somewhere along the road and attempt to eat you alive. Get the fear out of the shadow and into the light.

Lest we get too highfalutin in our theories and practices within the spectrum of leadership capabilities, it would be good for us to remember how the Apostles chose Judas' replacement. They drew straws. Well, what do you think of that? No risk assessment, no goals or priorities, just a bunch of lots. One was a bit different in length than the others. They trusted the Holy Spirit to guide the action and got on with life afterwards.

I know there have been many meetings I have wished we would have resorted to the apostolic selection medium to get the work done. In the end, my heart and mind were able to grow through the process, a feature that the drawing of straws does not immediately present. I think the take-away on this practice (of drawing straws) is that any decision can really be acceptable provided that you have the people behind it willing to work with whatever comes up as a result of making it. If you have the right group of people behind a decision, then even the wrong decision can work out for the good.

That belief, my brothers and sisters, is exactly the belief we need to work toward in our groups and teams. We need to develop our teams and groups to the point where we feel comfortable with the people in them. We trust them immensely. We trust them so much that we are sure that even if we choose wrong and make mistakes, that it will all work out because of who those people are; and of course who God is as well. That perfect trust; that perfect love, casts out all fear.

A leader recognizes that when it is all said and done, no matter the decision that is made it is really the group living the execution of the decision that makes all the difference.

Connectivity Toolbox
—Stuff for your Journal

- Make a list of twelve recent decisions you have made—in your journal. Place an "x" next to those decisions that you feel worked out well. Write the word "frozen" next to those decisions that you have made, but have done nothing else since deciding. Are you frozen because you are waiting for something to happen that is out of your control or are you frozen because of something in your own life?
- List some decisions you have made in life that have been a complete and utter failure. In your journal next to the failure, write what it is that you have learned from that failure and how you have placed "work-arounds" in your life to deal with those failures in the future.
- Share with your group how you usually make a personal decision. Make sure to list out the components of your decision making process in your journal so you can share them without forgetting something. Be sure to take notes on observations you make from other peoples' examples.
- Have you ever made a decision like the Apostles did? Sort of a "Hail Mary" decision? If so talk about it with your group. Talk about how it worked out.
- Do you feel comfortable enough with this group to make that kind of decision with this group of people? If not, why? How can you get the group—yourself included—to the place where you can all feel comfortable enough to move on past this kind of decision? Make some notes about this in your journal.
- What was your hardest life decision? Share this with your group.
- What was your easiest life decision? Share this with your group.
- Write a note to everyone in your group that studied this handbook and thank them for doing this work with you.
- Workbook pages at: http://feedmysheepleadmysheep.blogspot.com/

www.ingramcontent.com/pod-product-compliance
Lightning Source LLC
Chambersburg PA
CBHW071445150426
43191CB00008B/1249